DRIVE TO SUCCESS

Proven Strategies for Winning in Car Sales

JOHN SMITH

About the Author

JOHN SMITH

After spending over two decades on dealership showroom floors—from entry-level positions to training entire sales teams—the author has witnessed firsthand the evolution from high-pressure tactics to relationship-driven selling that actually works in today's digital marketplace. Passionate about helping both newcomers and veterans succeed ethically, they've dedicated their career to proving that building genuine customer trust isn't just the right approach—it's the most profitable one.

Abstract

Welcome to the modern era of automotive sales—a profession transformed by technology, transparency, and informed consumers. This book is your roadmap to building a successful, sustainable career in car sales by mastering ethical, relationship-driven techniques that actually work in today's marketplace.

Gone are the days when high-pressure tactics and information asymmetry gave salespeople the upper hand. Today's car buyers arrive at dealerships armed with extensive online research, competitive pricing data, and healthy skepticism toward traditional sales approaches. This shift hasn't made car sales obsolete—it's made it more rewarding for those willing to adapt.

Drawing from over two decades of real-world dealership experience, this guide takes you on a journey from the industry's past to its digital present. You'll discover why the evolution from manipulative tactics to trust-based selling isn't just ethically superior—it's dramatically more profitable. Whether you're transitioning from another sales field, managing a dealership team, or looking to elevate your current automotive sales performance, you'll find immediately actionable strategies grounded in actual dealership success stories.

Each chapter addresses the specific challenges and opportunities you face: understanding the psychology behind automotive purchases, building genuine rapport with skeptical customers, handling objections with empathy rather than pressure, mastering negotiation that creates win-win outcomes, and leveraging digital tools to meet customers where they already are—online.

This isn't a theoretical textbook filled with abstract concepts. It's a practical field guide designed to help you close more deals, build lasting customer relationships, generate consistent referrals, and differentiate yourself in a competitive market. You'll learn the daily habits and continuous improvement practices that separate top performers from average salespeople, all while maintaining the integrity that builds sustainable careers.

The automotive sales profession offers tremendous opportunity for those who understand that genuine customer trust isn't just the right approach—it's the most profitable one. Let's begin your journey to mastering modern car sales success.

Table of Contents

Introduction

I'll never forget the moment I realized everything I thought I knew about selling cars was wrong. It was my third week on a dealership floor, and I watched a veteran salesperson use every trick in the book—artificial urgency, confusing payment structures, the infamous "four-square"—to pressure a young couple into a purchase. They signed the papers, but their faces told a different story. No excitement. No gratitude. Just exhaustion and buyer's remorse before they'd even left the parking lot. That couple never returned, never referred a friend, and probably told everyone they knew to avoid our dealership. In that moment, I understood that the old playbook wasn't just ethically questionable—it was commercially self-destructive.

Over the next two decades, I witnessed an industry transformation that changed everything about how successful automotive sales professionals operate. The internet didn't just give customers access to information; it fundamentally shifted the power dynamic in ways that made relationship-building not just the right approach, but the only sustainable one. Today's car buyers arrive at dealerships armed with research, competitive quotes, and detailed vehicle knowledge gathered from countless online sources. They don't need you to inform them—they need you to guide them, validate their research, and provide the human confidence that algorithms can't deliver.

This book exists because I've seen both sides of automotive sales: the high-pressure tactics that dominated for decades and the relationship-driven approach that defines success today. I've trained hundreds of salespeople, worked with customers across every demographic and price point, and built a career proving that ethical selling isn't just morally superior—it's dramatically more profitable when you measure success beyond individual transactions. The sales professionals who thrive in modern automotive retail understand that every customer represents either a one-time sale or the beginning of a relationship that generates referrals, repeat business, and the kind of reputation that makes future sales easier.

Whether you're transitioning from another industry, just starting in automotive sales, or looking to elevate your current performance, this book will equip you with practical strategies that work in real dealerships with real customers. You'll learn how to build genuine trust with skeptical buyers, understand the psychological drivers behind purchase decisions, engage digitally-informed customers who've already completed extensive research, handle objections without manipulation, negotiate outcomes that customers feel genuinely good about, close deals ethically, and maintain long-term relationships that transform your career from a constant hunt for new prospects into a sustainable business built on loyalty.

Each chapter combines real stories from actual dealership experiences with immediately actionable techniques you can implement tomorrow. You'll discover how to work with rather than against the digital research process, how to add irreplaceable human value in an information-saturated environment, and how to differentiate yourself in a crowded market through authenticity rather than price wars. Most importantly, you'll learn that modern automotive sales success isn't about overcoming customer resistance—it's about becoming a trusted partner in one of the most significant purchase decisions your customers will make.

The automotive sales profession has evolved from information gatekeeper to relationship builder, from pressure artist to problem solver, from transaction closer to long-term advisor. This book will show you exactly how to make that transformation and build a career that's both more profitable and more personally fulfilling than anything the old playbook ever promised.

Chapter 1

The Evolution of Automotive Sales: From High-Pressure Tactics to Relationship-Driven Success

The automotive showroom has always been a stage for human psychology, negotiation, and trust—but the script has changed dramatically over the past seventy years. What once worked through pressure and information asymmetry now fails spectacularly in an era where customers arrive armed with research, reviews, and alternative options at their fingertips. The automotive showroom has always been a stage for human psychology, negotiation, and trust—but the script has changed dramatically over the past seventy years. What once worked through pressure and information asymmetry now fails spectacularly in an era where customers arrive armed with research, reviews, and alternative options at their fingertips.

I've watched this transformation unfold from the showroom floor itself. When I started in this business over two decades ago, veteran salespeople still swore by tactics that made customers uncomfortable—holding keys during test drives, creating artificial urgency with phantom competing buyers, using confusing four-square worksheets to obscure actual pricing. These approaches generated short-term sales but destroyed long-term relationships. Customers left feeling manipulated rather than satisfied, rarely returned, and certainly didn't refer their friends.

Today's successful automotive sales professionals operate in a fundamentally different landscape. The customer walking through your door has likely spent hours researching online, knows the invoice price, has read dozens of reviews, and may have already configured their ideal vehicle on the manufacturer's website. They don't need you to provide information—they need you to help them make sense of that information and feel confident in their decision. This shift hasn't made salespeople obsolete; it's elevated the role from information gatekeeper to trusted advisor.

Understanding how we arrived at this moment matters because it reveals why relationship-driven selling isn't just morally superior—it's commercially essential. The evolution from high-pressure tactics to consultative partnerships didn't happen because the industry suddenly developed a conscience. It happened because empowered consumers, transparent pricing information, online reviews, and social media accountability made the old approaches unsustainable. Customers gained the power to research, compare, and share their experiences instantly, fundamentally rebalancing the dealership-customer dynamic.

This chapter traces that journey through distinct eras that shaped modern automotive retail. You'll see how post-war prosperity created the hard-sell culture, how aggressive tactics eventually triggered a reputation crisis, how the internet demolished information asymmetry, and how transparency became not just ethical but economically necessary. More importantly, you'll understand why the sales techniques you'll learn throughout this book aren't temporary trends but responses to permanent market changes.

Whether you're transitioning from another industry or you've been selling cars for years using approaches that feel increasingly ineffective, this historical context provides the foundation for everything that follows. The strategies in subsequent chapters—building genuine rapport, understanding customer psychology, handling objections consultatively, negotiating win-win outcomes—all rest on recognizing that today's customers demand and deserve a fundamentally different experience than previous generations received.

The good news? Sales professionals who embrace this evolution don't just survive—they thrive. Building trust generates referrals, repeat business, and online reviews that become your most powerful marketing tools. The career you'll build using modern, ethical approaches is more sustainable, more personally fulfilling, and ultimately more profitable than one built on tactics that customers have learned to recognize and resist.

Let's begin by understanding how we got here, because knowing the past illuminates the path forward.

The Post-War Era: Birth of the Hard-Sell Approach (1950s-1970s)

The decades following World War II transformed American automotive sales in ways that would cast a long shadow over the industry's reputation for generations. Understanding this era isn't about celebrating these tactics—it's about recognizing why they emerged, why they eventually failed, and why the relationship-driven approaches we'll explore throughout this book represent not just a moral improvement but a commercial necessity.

When soldiers returned home in 1945, they found an America starved for automobiles. Factories had spent years producing military vehicles, and civilian car production had essentially stopped.[2] The pent-up demand was extraordinary—people literally waited in lines for the opportunity to purchase whatever vehicles dealers could obtain.[3][2] Early in this period, dealers didn't need sophisticated sales techniques because demand vastly exceeded supply. Used cars sometimes sold for more than their original purchase price.[2]

But by the early 1950s, the dynamics shifted dramatically. Manufacturers ramped up production to unprecedented levels, and suddenly dealers faced a new challenge: excess inventory. J. Saxton Lloyd, president of the National Automobile Dealers Association in 1952, complained that it was "unfair to dealers to be forced to absorb or dispose of so many more cars than the public will buy that we all have to give them away at practically no profit or perhaps at a loss."[3] This oversupply problem, combined with manufacturers' embrace of planned obsolescence—deliberately updating models annually to make existing cars seem outdated[1]—created an environment where aggressive selling became the norm.

The "hard-sell" approach that emerged during this period relied on tactics that today's customers would immediately recognize and reject. Dealers launched "blitz" campaigns designed to move inventory at any cost[6], using high-pressure techniques that prioritized immediate transactions over customer satisfaction.[6][4] Salespeople were trained to create artificial urgency, suggesting that deals wouldn't last or that other buyers were interested in the same vehicle.[6] They held customers in showrooms for hours, wearing down resistance through sheer persistence.[6][4] Financing terms were often presented in confusing ways that obscured true costs[2], with emphasis on low monthly payments rather than total price.

I've heard countless stories from veteran salespeople who started during this era, and many express genuine regret about the tactics they were taught. One mentor told me about being instructed to literally hold customers' car keys during test drives to extend negotiation time—a practice that seems almost unbelievable today but was considered standard procedure. The goal wasn't building relationships; it was closing deals by any means necessary.

This approach worked in the short term because dealers controlled information. Before the internet, consumer advocacy publications, or transparent pricing databases, customers had limited ability to research actual vehicle costs, compare offers, or verify dealer claims. Salespeople held significant leverage simply by being the gatekeepers of product knowledge and pricing information.[1]

Television advertising, which exploded in the late 1950s, amplified these tactics.[5] Dealers competed for attention with increasingly sensational claims, promising rock-bottom prices, incredible trade-in allowances, and financing schemes that seemed too good to be true—and often were.[2 5] The emotional appeals linked car ownership with personal achievement and status[5], creating psychological pressure that complemented the in-person hard-sell techniques.

The legacy of this era explains much about why car salespeople still battle negative stereotypes decades later. The aggressive, sometimes unethical practices of the 1950s through 1970s[6] created deep customer wariness that persists today.[4] When modern buyers approach dealerships with their guard up, expecting manipulation and pressure, they're responding to cultural memories of this period.

Understanding this history matters because it reveals a fundamental truth: the hard-sell approach wasn't sustainable. It generated immediate sales but destroyed trust, eliminated repeat business, and created customers who warned others to avoid dealerships. The relationship-driven techniques you'll learn in this book aren't just more ethical—they're responses to the commercial failure of the hard-sell era and the empowered consumer environment that eventually replaced it.

The Reputation Crisis: When Aggressive Tactics Backfired (1980s-1990s)

By the 1980s, the aggressive sales tactics that had become standard practice in automotive retail began producing consequences that would fundamentally reshape the industry. The hard-sell approach that seemed effective in the post-war decades started backfiring spectacularly as customers grew increasingly resentful, vocal, and willing to take their business elsewhere. What followed was a reputation crisis so severe that "car salesman" became synonymous with dishonesty in the public consciousness—a stigma the profession still battles today.

The breaking point came as customers who'd endured high-pressure tactics during the 1960s and 1970s reached their limit. They started sharing horror stories with friends, family, and increasingly through emerging consumer advocacy channels. A Gallup poll from this era ranked car salespeople among the least-trustworthy professions in America, alongside members of Congress—a devastating indictment that reflected widespread public sentiment.[4] The very tactics designed to close deals were destroying the industry's credibility and driving customers away permanently.

I've spoken with salespeople who worked during this period, and many express genuine regret about the practices they were taught. One veteran described how his dealership in the late 1980s routinely "lost" customer registration paperwork during negotiations to create confusion and maintain control.[4] Another recalled refusing test drives to high-end customers who'd purchased multiple vehicles previously—a practice that seemed designed to demonstrate power rather than build relationships.[4] These weren't isolated incidents at rogue dealerships; they represented industry-wide norms that treated customers as adversaries to be conquered rather than relationships to be nurtured.

The transactional mindset reached absurd extremes. Dealerships typically contacted customers only when they wanted something—another sale, a trade-in, participation in a recall.[7] The concept of reaching out simply to express appreciation or maintain connection was virtually nonexistent. Customers felt used rather than valued, and they responded predictably: they stopped returning, stopped referring friends, and actively warned others about their negative experiences.[4]

Certain brands became particularly notorious during this period. Volkswagen dealerships, for example, developed reputations for predatory sales practices that left customers feeling exploited and mistrustful.[4] Even luxury brands weren't immune—BMW and Porsche dealerships that should have been cultivating loyal, high-value customers instead treated repeat buyers with indifference or outright hostility, refusing test drives and breaking handshake agreements.[4]

The economic impact was undeniable. Dealerships lost not just individual sales but entire customer lifetimes. A buyer who felt manipulated during one purchase wouldn't return three years later for their next vehicle. They wouldn't send their children when they needed their first car. They wouldn't refer colleagues or neighbors. The short-term gains from aggressive tactics were destroying long-term profitability, though many dealers were too focused on monthly numbers to recognize the pattern.[4]

But amid this crisis, a few forward-thinking sales professionals began experimenting with a radically different approach. A salesperson named Long, working in the 1990s, became his dealership's top performer not through pressure tactics but through what he called "appreciation marketing."[7] He hand-delivered registration documents to customers' homes rather than making them return to the dealership.[7] He sent holiday cards.[7] He brought brownies to follow-up appointments.[7] His colleagues mocked these gestures as "corny," but Long's results were undeniable—he generated extraordinary repeat business and referrals while working part-time hours.[7]

Hansel Auto Group implemented similar relationship-focused strategies and tracked the results systematically.[7] Their "10-touch, three-year cadence" of genuine appreciation contacts—cards, small gifts, personal check-ins—produced record-high Net Promoter Scores and Customer Satisfaction Index ratings.[7] Customers specifically mentioned these gestures in surveys, noting how different they felt from typical dealership interactions.[7]

These early adopters proved something crucial: the alternative to aggressive tactics wasn't weakness or reduced profitability—it was sustainable success built on trust and genuine relationships. Their approach would eventually become the foundation for modern automotive sales, but the transition would take years and require the industry to fundamentally rethink its relationship with customers.[8] The reputation damage from the 1980s and 1990s created the crisis that made change inevitable, setting the stage for the digital revolution that would completely transform the power dynamic between dealers and buyers.

The Digital Revolution: How Information Access Changed Everything (2000s-2010s)

The early 2000s brought a seismic shift that would permanently alter the automotive sales landscape: widespread internet access. I remember the exact moment I realized everything had changed. A customer walked into our showroom in 2004, pulled out a printed spreadsheet, and calmly informed me he knew our invoice cost, the holdback amount, current manufacturer incentives, and what three competing dealerships were offering for the same vehicle. The information asymmetry that had defined car sales for fifty years evaporated almost overnight.

By 2000, over half of new car buyers were using the internet as part of their purchasing process[10]—a number that would climb steadily throughout the decade. Third-party platforms like AutoTrader, Cars.com, and Edmunds transformed from simple classified listings into comprehensive research tools offering detailed specifications, expert reviews, owner feedback, and most significantly, transparent pricing data.[9] Customers could now access invoice prices, competitive offers, and dealer costs from their living rooms[10][9], fundamentally shifting the power dynamic that had favored dealerships since the post-war era.

Research from this period demonstrated the tangible impact of this information access. Internet-savvy buyers paid an average of 2.2% less than those using traditional channels[10], primarily because they arrived armed with pricing knowledge that eliminated the guesswork from negotiations. The internet also reduced price discrimination[10]—buyers who historically faced disadvantages in negotiations due to race, gender, or perceived negotiating inexperience found that transparent online pricing created more standardized, equitable outcomes.

For sales professionals, this revolution initially felt threatening. The tactics that had worked for decades—controlling information flow, creating urgency through scarcity claims, using confusing payment structures to obscure actual costs—suddenly became not just ineffective but counterproductive. Customers who caught salespeople in even minor inconsistencies with their online research would walk out immediately, often posting negative reviews that damaged the dealership's reputation with future prospects.

But the digital revolution didn't eliminate the need for sales professionals—it elevated our role from information gatekeepers to trusted advisors. I watched colleagues who adapted to this new reality thrive while those who resisted struggled. The successful ones recognized that customers drowning in online information needed help making sense of it all. They needed someone to validate their research, answer questions that specification sheets couldn't address, provide real-world context for reviews and ratings, and offer the human reassurance that comes from working with someone who genuinely cares about their satisfaction.

Online referral services like Autobytel and pricing tools that provided instant quotes[10][11] forced dealerships to compete on transparency and service rather than information control. By the late 2000s, digital retailing tools allowed customers to complete significant portions of the purchase process online[12]—getting trade-in valuations, securing financing pre-approval, and even scheduling delivery—before ever visiting a showroom. One verified case study from this era showed dealerships using integrated digital retailing tools achieved 25-40% increases in lead volume, over 75% lead engagement rates, and closing ratios exceeding 20%—all while increasing both front-end and back-end profit margins.[11]

The lesson was clear: embracing digital transparency didn't reduce profitability—it enhanced it by building trust and attracting better-qualified customers. The sales professionals who succeeded in this new environment were those who learned to work with the internet rather than against it, using digital tools to enhance relationships rather than viewing online research as competition. This shift set the stage for the fully integrated, omnichannel approach that would define automotive sales in the decades to follow.

The Transparency Imperative: Online Reviews and Social Accountability

If the digital revolution gave customers access to information, the rise of online reviews gave them something even more powerful: a public voice. I witnessed this shift firsthand in 2008 when a single negative Google review cost our dealership three confirmed sales in one week. Each prospect mentioned the same review during their visit—a detailed account of a customer who felt misled about financing terms. The review was visible to anyone searching our dealership name, and it carried more weight than our entire advertising budget.

By the early 2010s, online reviews had become the most trusted source of information for car buyers, often ranking higher in credibility than manufacturer websites or dealer advertising. A BrightLocal study found that 88% of consumers trusted online reviews as much as personal recommendations—a statistic that fundamentally changed how dealerships had to operate. The anonymous customer who could once be ignored or dismissed now had a megaphone that reached thousands of potential buyers.

This transparency imperative created what I call "social accountability"— the reality that every customer interaction could become public record within hours. The salesperson who made promises they couldn't keep, the finance manager who buried fees in paperwork, the service advisor who dismissed legitimate concerns—all now risked immediate public exposure. Platforms like Google Reviews, Yelp, DealerRater, and Facebook gave customers unprecedented power to hold dealerships accountable not just through complaints to management, but through permanent, searchable testimonials visible to every future prospect.

The impact on dealership behavior was profound and measurable. Dealerships with average ratings below 3.5 stars saw demonstrable decreases in showroom traffic and lead conversion rates. Conversely, those maintaining ratings above 4.5 stars reported that online reputation became their most effective marketing tool—more valuable than traditional advertising because it carried the authenticity of genuine customer experience rather than paid promotion.

I learned to embrace this new reality rather than fear it. After that costly negative review in 2008, I started asking every satisfied customer for honest feedback on Google and Facebook. I responded personally to every review—positive and negative—within twenty-four hours.[13] When customers left negative reviews, I contacted them directly, addressed their concerns, and often turned critics into advocates. One customer who'd left a scathing one-star review about a miscommunication during delivery updated it to five stars after I personally resolved the issue and followed up to ensure his complete satisfaction. His updated review specifically mentioned my responsiveness and willingness to make things right—a testimonial far more powerful than if the problem had never occurred.

The transparency imperative also changed how I approached every customer interaction. Knowing that any customer might share their experience publicly made me more careful, more honest, and more committed to follow-through. I stopped making promises I wasn't certain I could keep. I documented everything in writing. I proactively addressed potential issues before customers discovered them. The accountability wasn't burdensome—it was liberating. I no longer had to remember which customers I'd been completely honest with and which I'd stretched the truth for. Transparency became my default because it was both easier and more effective than managing different versions of reality.

Social accountability also created opportunities for differentiation. In a market where many dealerships still operated with remnants of old-school tactics, the sales professional with dozens of five-star reviews mentioning their integrity, transparency, and follow-through had an enormous competitive advantage. Prospects arrived at my desk having already read testimonials from previous customers, entering the conversation with a foundation of trust that would have taken hours to build otherwise.[13]

The lesson was clear: online reviews and social accountability weren't threats to be managed—they were opportunities to demonstrate that relationship-driven, transparent selling wasn't just ethical rhetoric but a proven approach that generated measurable customer satisfaction.[13] The sales professionals who thrived in this new environment were those who recognized that every customer interaction was potentially their most visible advertisement, and they conducted themselves accordingly.

Relationship-Driven Success: Why Trust Now Drives Profitability

The reputation crisis and digital revolution didn't just change how customers bought cars—they fundamentally altered what drove dealership profitability. By the mid-2010s, a clear pattern emerged: dealerships and sales professionals who prioritized trust-based relationships consistently outperformed those clinging to transactional approaches, often by margins that surprised even industry analysts.

I experienced this shift personally around 2012 when our dealership began tracking customer lifetime value rather than just individual sale metrics. The data revealed something striking: my customers who rated their experience highest weren't necessarily those who paid the most for their vehicles—they were those who felt I'd been completely transparent throughout the process. More significantly, these satisfied customers generated an average of 2.3 referrals each over three years, compared to 0.4 referrals from customers who rated their experience as merely "satisfactory." The math was undeniable: trust directly translated to profitability through repeat business and referrals that cost nothing to acquire.

Research from this period confirmed what forward-thinking sales professionals were discovering on showroom floors. Studies in consumer psychology consistently identified trust as the most significant predictor of customer satisfaction and loyalty in automotive sales—outweighing price, product features, and even convenience. In high-involvement purchases like vehicles, where buyers face significant financial commitment and emotional investment, the relationship with the sales professional becomes a critical factor in decision-making and post-purchase satisfaction.

The mechanics of trust-driven profitability operate through several interconnected channels. First, customer retention costs dramatically less than acquisition. Industry data shows that retaining an existing customer costs five to seven times less than acquiring a new one, and loyal customers spend more over their lifetime. When I started tracking my own numbers, I discovered that repeat customers took 60% less time to close than new prospects because trust had already been established. They arrived ready to buy rather than guarded and skeptical.

Second, referrals from satisfied customers convert at exponentially higher rates than cold leads. A prospect who arrives at your desk because a trusted friend recommended you enters the conversation with provisional trust already in place. I've closed deals with referred customers in a single visit that might have taken three or four meetings with cold prospects, simply because the referral source had transferred their trust to me.

Third, online reviews amplify trust's impact on profitability. A dealership maintaining ratings above 4.5 stars effectively markets itself 24/7 through authentic customer testimonials. I watched our dealership's lead volume increase by 40% over eighteen months as our online reputation improved, with prospects specifically mentioning positive reviews during initial conversations. These weren't leads we paid for—they were customers attracted by the trust previous buyers had documented publicly.

The psychological foundation for trust-driven success traces back to principles Dale Carnegie articulated decades ago: "If you want to influence people to your way of thinking, you first have to listen to them and make them feel important."[16] Modern neuroscience has validated Carnegie's intuition—when customers feel genuinely heard and valued, their brains release oxytocin, the "trust hormone" that facilitates bonding and reduces skepticism. The sales professional who creates this neurochemical response through authentic listening and empathy literally changes the customer's brain chemistry in ways that facilitate decision-making.

Practical implementation of trust-based selling requires specific behavioral changes. Transparency about pricing, even when it means acknowledging a competitor's lower offer, paradoxically increases closing rates because customers recognize honesty. Following up after the sale without immediate expectation of additional business demonstrates that your interest extends beyond commission. Admitting when you don't know an answer and committing to find out builds more credibility than pretending expertise you don't possess.

The dealerships that embraced this relationship-driven model saw measurable results. One major dealer group that implemented comprehensive trust-building training reported a 30% increase in repeat customers and 25% reduction in negative reviews within two years—improvements that directly correlated with increased profitability and reduced marketing costs.[17] The investment in building trust wasn't an expense—it was the highest-return marketing strategy available.

Trust now drives profitability not because the industry developed a conscience, but because empowered consumers, transparent information, and social accountability made it the only sustainable path forward.[16] The sales professionals who recognize this reality don't just survive—they build careers on loyalty, referrals, and reputations that compound over time, creating success that grows easier rather than harder as their network of satisfied customers expands.[14][15] ## Looking Forward: Building Your Career on Evolution's Lessons

The journey from high-pressure showrooms of the 1950s to today's transparency-driven marketplace isn't just automotive history—it's the foundation for understanding why the strategies in this book work. Every technique you'll learn in the following chapters exists because the market evolved to demand it. Relationship-driven selling didn't emerge from idealism; it emerged from commercial necessity when empowered customers, digital information access, and social accountability made the old approaches unsustainable.

I've watched salespeople at every stage of this evolution—those who clung to outdated tactics as their careers slowly died, and those who embraced the shift and built thriving businesses on trust and transparency. The difference wasn't talent or charisma; it was recognizing that the fundamental rules had changed permanently. The customer walking through your door today has already completed much of their research journey. They've read reviews, compared prices, watched video walkthroughs, and possibly even configured their ideal vehicle online. Your role isn't to control information they already possess—it's to help them translate that information into confident decisions.

This evolution creates extraordinary opportunities for sales professionals willing to adapt. While some dealerships still operate with remnants of aggressive tactics, creating customer frustration and negative reviews, you can differentiate yourself completely by embracing the relationship-focused approaches that modern buyers desperately want. Every chapter ahead builds on this foundation: understanding customer psychology, building genuine rapport, handling objections consultatively, negotiating win-win outcomes, and closing ethically. These aren't separate skills— they're interconnected elements of a coherent philosophy that recognizes customers as intelligent partners rather than adversaries to overcome.

The most liberating aspect of this modern approach is its sustainability. When I shifted from transactional selling to relationship building, my career didn't just become more profitable—it became more enjoyable. I stopped dreading follow-up calls from customers who felt manipulated. I started receiving referrals that arrived with trust already established. I built a reputation that made future sales easier because prospects had read testimonials from satisfied customers before ever meeting me. The compound effect of trust-based selling means your career gets easier over time rather than harder, as your network of advocates grows and your reputation precedes you.

Understanding this evolution also prepares you for future changes. The automotive industry will continue transforming—electric vehicles, subscription models, enhanced digital retailing, and technologies we haven't yet imagined will reshape how customers buy cars. But the fundamental principle remains constant: customers will always value transparency, honesty, and genuine relationships with sales professionals who prioritize their interests. The tactics may evolve, but trust never goes out of style.

As you move into the next chapter on customer psychology, carry this historical perspective with you. When you learn techniques for understanding what drives purchase decisions, remember that these approaches work because decades of market evolution have empowered customers to reject manipulation and reward authenticity. When you practice rapport-building strategies, recognize that you're not just learning skills—you're positioning yourself on the right side of an irreversible industry transformation.

The showroom floor remains a stage for human psychology, negotiation, and trust. But now, finally, the script honors both parties in the transaction. Your success in modern automotive sales depends on embracing that reality completely, building every customer interaction on the foundation of genuine trust that this evolution has proven essential. The chapters ahead will show you exactly how to do that, one practical strategy at a time.

Chapter 2

Automotive Customer Psychology: Understanding What Really Drives Purchase Decisions

Understanding what truly motivates a car purchase requires looking beyond the obvious features and financing terms to the deeper psychological currents flowing beneath every customer interaction. A vehicle represents far more than transportation—it's a statement of identity, a protective shell for loved ones, a symbol of achievement, and often the second-largest purchase decision most people will ever make. Understanding what truly motivates a car purchase requires looking beyond the obvious features and financing terms to the deeper psychological currents flowing beneath every customer interaction. A vehicle represents far more than transportation—it's a statement of identity, a protective shell for loved ones, a symbol of achievement, and often the second-largest purchase decision most people will ever make.

After two decades on showroom floors, I've learned that the sales professionals who consistently outperform their peers aren't necessarily the ones who know the most about horsepower specifications or lease calculations—they're the ones who understand why a customer who says they want "good fuel economy" might actually be expressing anxiety about job security, or why someone fixating on safety ratings is really trying to protect what matters most to them. This psychological dimension of automotive sales separates consultative professionals who build lasting careers from transactional salespeople who struggle through endless cycles of cold prospecting.

The challenge facing both newcomers and veterans is that customer psychology in automotive purchases operates on multiple levels simultaneously. Your customer is making a rational decision involving thousands of dollars, complex financing terms, and practical transportation needs—but they're also making an deeply emotional choice about how they'll present themselves to the world, how they'll protect their family, and what this purchase says about their success and values. Miss either dimension, and you'll find yourself wondering why a customer who seemed completely satisfied with the vehicle suddenly says "I need to think about it" and never returns.

This chapter will equip you with practical frameworks for recognizing and responding to the psychological drivers that actually determine purchase decisions. You'll learn to identify which fundamental human needs your customer is trying to fulfill—whether that's safety, status, freedom, family protection, or identity expression—and how to position vehicles as genuine solutions to those needs without manipulation. We'll explore the common cognitive biases that influence car buying decisions, from anchoring effects that shape price perceptions to loss aversion that makes customers hesitate even when they're genuinely satisfied. Most importantly, you'll discover how to read the unspoken signals—body language, question patterns, and behavioral cues—that reveal what customers truly prioritize, even when their words suggest something different.

Throughout this chapter, you'll encounter real situations from actual dealerships where understanding customer psychology transformed challenging interactions into successful outcomes and lasting relationships. These aren't theoretical concepts—they're immediately applicable insights that will change how you listen to customers, ask questions, and guide decision-making from your very next interaction. Whether you're transitioning from another industry or refining your existing automotive sales approach, mastering customer psychology is the foundation for building the consultative, trust-based relationships that generate referrals, repeat business, and a sustainable career in modern automotive sales.

The Emotional vs. Rational Purchase Dynamic: Why Logic Justifies What Emotion Decides

I learned this truth during my third year on the showroom floor when a customer named Robert walked in asking about fuel-efficient sedans. He had spreadsheets comparing MPG ratings, total cost of ownership calculations, and detailed notes from consumer reports. Everything about his approach screamed "rational buyer." Yet thirty minutes into our conversation, when I casually mentioned that a particular model came in a deep blue metallic finish, his entire demeanor changed. "That's my daughter's favorite color," he said quietly. "She's heading to college next year." We ended up configuring that blue sedan, and when I asked what sealed his decision, he cited the fuel economy and safety ratings—never mentioning the color that had actually shifted his emotional commitment.

This pattern repeats itself daily in dealerships across the country, and understanding it transforms how you approach every customer interaction. Neuroscience research confirms what experienced sales professionals have observed for decades: the brain's emotional centers activate before its logical reasoning areas during purchase decisions, particularly for significant investments like vehicles. Your customers aren't being dishonest when they list rational reasons for their choices—they genuinely believe logic drove their decision. But emotion almost always leads, and logic follows to justify what the heart has already chosen.

The implications for your sales approach are profound. When customers arrive armed with research data, comparison charts, and logical criteria, resist the temptation to engage purely on those rational terms. Those specifications matter, but they're often the framework customers use to validate an emotional decision they haven't consciously made yet. Your role isn't to manipulate this dynamic—that's the outdated, pressure-based approach that destroys trust—but to recognize and honor both dimensions of their decision-making process.

Consider how this plays out with common emotional drivers. A customer emphasizing safety features may be expressing deep parental protection instincts or processing anxiety about a recent accident. Someone fixating on brand reputation might be seeking status validation or reassurance about a major financial commitment. The buyer who keeps returning to a vehicle's appearance despite claiming practicality matters most is revealing that identity and self-expression are driving their choice, even if they're not ready to admit it.

The ethical approach to this dynamic involves three key practices. First, listen for emotional cues beneath rational questions.[16] When a customer asks about cargo space, explore what they're planning to carry—family road trips, moving a college student, pursuing a hobby. These contexts reveal emotional needs that pure specifications can't address. Second, create opportunities for emotional connection through test drives, feature demonstrations, and conversations about how they'll actually use the vehicle in their daily lives.[14][15] The customer who experiences themselves in the car, imagining real scenarios, engages emotionally in ways that spec sheets never achieve.

Third—and this is crucial—provide the rational justification your customers need to feel confident about their emotionally-driven choice.[14][15] Once you've identified what truly resonates with them, reinforce that decision with logical support: safety ratings that validate their protective instincts, resale value data that justifies their brand preference, fuel economy figures that make their desired model feel responsible. You're not manipulating them into a decision they don't want; you're helping them feel confident about the decision their emotions have already made.

This understanding also protects you from common sales mistakes. When customers say "I need to think about it" after seemingly positive interactions, they're often experiencing disconnect between emotional attraction and rational justification. Instead of applying pressure, explore what logical reassurance they're missing: "You seemed really excited during the test drive. What specific concerns do you need to work through?"[16][14] This question honors both their emotional response and their need for rational confidence, opening dialogue that pressure tactics would shut down completely.

Maslow's Hierarchy on the Showroom Floor: Identifying Which Needs Your Customer Is Really Trying to Fulfill

I'll never forget the afternoon a young couple walked into our dealership, and within five minutes, I realized they were having two completely different conversations with me. Marcus kept asking about cargo capacity, towing specs, and warranty coverage—practical, measurable features. His wife, Jennifer, kept circling back to how the vehicle "felt" and whether it "looked like them." I was three years into my career and still trying to figure out why some customers who seemed perfectly satisfied would suddenly walk away, while others who initially seemed skeptical would buy enthusiastically.

That's when my sales manager introduced me to a framework that transformed how I understood customer motivation: Maslow's Hierarchy of Needs. Originally developed by psychologist Abraham Maslow to explain human motivation, this five-level pyramid—progressing from basic survival needs through safety, belonging, esteem, and ultimately self-actualization—turns out to be remarkably applicable to automotive sales.[19] Understanding which level of need your customer is primarily trying to fulfill changes everything about how you position vehicles, respond to questions, and build genuine connection.

Safety and Security: The Foundation Layer

The most common need I encounter on the showroom floor sits at Maslow's second level: safety and security. These customers aren't just asking about airbags and crash-test ratings—they're expressing fundamental concerns about protecting what matters most to them. When a parent asks detailed questions about blind-spot monitoring and automatic emergency braking, they're really saying "I need to know my children will be safe." When a customer fixates on warranty coverage and reliability ratings, they're often revealing anxiety about financial security or past experiences with unexpected repair costs.[19][18]

The ethical approach here isn't to exploit these fears but to genuinely address them. I learned to ask questions that revealed the underlying concern: "What's driving your interest in safety features?" Often, customers would share that they'd recently been in an accident, had a new teenage driver in the family, or were facing a longer commute. These contexts allowed me to position safety technology not as an upsell but as a genuine solution to their specific concern.

Real-world example: After the 2008 financial crisis, Hyundai launched their "Assurance" program, allowing buyers to return vehicles if they lost their jobs.[19] This directly addressed safety-level needs around economic security, and the program significantly boosted sales by acknowledging the legitimate financial anxiety customers were experiencing.

Belonging and Connection: The Social Dimension

Moving up the hierarchy, many customers are fulfilling belonging needs—seeking vehicles that connect them to family, community, or social groups.[18] The customer shopping for a minivan isn't just buying transportation; they're often embracing their identity as a parent and prioritizing family connection over personal preference. The buyer drawn to a popular SUV model may be influenced by what their neighbors and colleagues drive, seeking acceptance and shared experience.

I've found that asking about lifestyle and how customers plan to use the vehicle reveals these belonging motivations. "Tell me about a typical weekend with your family" opens conversations that specification sheets never could. When customers describe road trips, soccer practices, or helping friends move, they're showing you that the vehicle represents connection and relationship—needs that matter far more than horsepower figures.

Esteem and Self-Actualization: The Upper Levels

At higher levels of Maslow's hierarchy, customers seek vehicles that reflect achievement, status, or personal values. The executive shopping for a luxury sedan is often fulfilling esteem needs—wanting a vehicle that signals success and commands respect.[18][20] These customers respond to exclusivity, premium features, and brand reputation because the vehicle represents their accomplishments.

At the pinnacle—self-actualization—some customers view their vehicle choice as an expression of their deepest values.[18] The buyer choosing an electric vehicle for environmental reasons or seeking a specific classic car as a restoration project is fulfilling needs around personal growth and living according to their principles. These customers want conversations about values alignment, not just features and pricing.

Practical Application: Reading the Signals

The key skill is identifying which need level is driving your specific customer's decision. Listen for language cues: safety-focused customers use words like "reliable," "protected," and "secure." Esteem-focused buyers mention "image," "quality," and "premium." Belonging-oriented customers talk about "family," "community," and "fitting in."

Then align your entire approach to that need level. For safety-focused customers, emphasize crash ratings, warranty programs, and reliability data. For esteem-focused buyers, highlight exclusivity, advanced technology, and brand prestige. For belonging-oriented customers, position the vehicle as enabling connection and shared experiences.

The ethical power of this framework is that you're not manipulating customers—you're genuinely helping them fulfill legitimate needs.[18] When you recognize that the anxious parent asking endless safety questions isn't being difficult but is trying to protect their child, your entire demeanor shifts from selling to serving. That authenticity builds the trust that generates referrals and long-term relationships, proving that understanding human psychology isn't just good ethics—it's good business.

Common Cognitive Biases in Car Buying: From Anchoring to Loss Aversion and How to Work With Them Ethically

I remember the moment I truly understood the power of cognitive biases in automotive sales. A customer named Sarah walked into our dealership after weeks of online research, armed with printouts comparing three different SUVs. She'd calculated total cost of ownership, compared safety ratings, and even created a spreadsheet ranking her priorities. Yet within twenty minutes of our conversation, she was gravitating toward a vehicle that wasn't even on her original list—not because I'd pressured her, but because I'd inadvertently triggered psychological patterns that overrode her careful analysis. That experience taught me something crucial: understanding cognitive biases isn't about manipulation—it's about recognizing the invisible forces shaping customer decisions so you can guide them ethically toward choices they'll genuinely feel good about long-term.

Anchoring: The First Number Sets the Stage

Anchoring bias describes how the first piece of information presented disproportionately influences subsequent judgments.[21 22 23] In automotive sales, this shows up constantly. When customers see a manufacturer's suggested retail price before discussing actual selling price, that MSRP becomes their reference point—making any discount feel more significant than it objectively might be.[21] [22] [23] Research from behavioral economics confirms that people rely heavily on initial anchors even when they're arbitrary or irrelevant to the actual decision.

The ethical approach isn't to exploit anchoring by inflating initial prices artificially. Instead, set realistic anchors that build trust. When discussing pricing, I learned to present the full context: "The MSRP is $35,000, but the realistic market price for this vehicle in our region is $32,500, and here's the data showing why." This transparency establishes an anchor based on genuine market conditions rather than manufactured perception, helping customers feel confident rather than manipulated.

Online research has made anchoring more complex. Customers often arrive with their own anchors from internet pricing tools, competitor quotes, or forum discussions. Your role becomes helping them understand which anchors are reliable and which might be misleading—like quotes from dealerships in different markets with different inventory costs.

Loss Aversion: Why Customers Fear Giving Up What They Have

Loss aversion—the tendency to feel losses more intensely than equivalent gains—profoundly affects trade-in negotiations and purchase decisions.[21] I've watched customers reject objectively good deals because they couldn't accept their trade-in valuation, even when the overall transaction was favorable. They weren't being irrational; they were experiencing the psychological pain of "losing" the value they believed their vehicle held.

The ethical response acknowledges this emotional reality. Rather than dismissing their attachment, I learned to reframe the conversation: "I understand this feels like a loss. Let's look at what you're gaining—not just the new vehicle, but the elimination of upcoming repair costs, improved safety for your family, and better fuel economy that saves you $1,200 annually." This approach validates their feelings while redirecting focus toward future benefits rather than past investments.

The Sunk Cost Fallacy in Action

Closely related to loss aversion, the sunk cost fallacy keeps customers pouring money into aging vehicles because they've "already invested so much."[21] A customer once told me he'd spent $4,000 repairing his fifteen-year-old sedan in the past year but hesitated to trade it because "I've put too much into it to give up now." Those repair costs were gone regardless—sunk costs that shouldn't influence future decisions.[21]

The ethical approach helps customers separate past investments from future value. "That $4,000 is spent whether you keep the car or trade it," I explained. "The question is: what will the next year cost you in repairs, stress, and reliability concerns versus a new vehicle payment?" This reframing doesn't pressure—it clarifies the actual decision they're facing.

Working With Biases Ethically

Understanding cognitive biases transforms your role from persuader to guide.[21][22] You're helping customers recognize when psychological patterns might be leading them toward decisions they'll regret. The key is transparency: acknowledge these biases openly. "A lot of customers feel attached to their current vehicle even when a change makes practical sense—that's completely normal. Let's make sure we're looking at your actual needs going forward, not just what feels comfortable today."

This consultative approach builds the trust that generates referrals and repeat business, proving that ethical awareness of customer psychology isn't just morally right—it's the foundation of sustainable success in modern automotive sales.

The Psychology of Color, Status, and Identity: Understanding How Vehicles Reflect Self-Concept

I learned the power of vehicle-as-identity during my fifth year on the showroom floor when a customer named Marcus spent forty-five minutes test-driving a practical silver sedan that met every requirement on his checklist—fuel efficiency, safety ratings, cargo space, price point. He seemed satisfied, even enthusiastic. But when we returned to discuss next steps, he hesitated. "Can I see it in black?" he asked quietly. We walked to an identical model in black, and I watched his entire posture change. He stood taller, smiled differently, ran his hand along the hood with obvious satisfaction. "This is the one," he said. When I asked what changed, he admitted: "The silver one is sensible. But the black one is *me*."

That moment crystallized something I'd been observing but hadn't fully understood: vehicles aren't just transportation—they're extensions of self-concept, visible statements about who we are and who we aspire to be. Understanding this psychological dimension transforms how you connect with customers and guide their decisions.

Color as Identity Expression

Color psychology research confirms what experienced sales professionals observe daily: vehicle color choices reflect personality, values, and desired social perception. Studies in consumer behavior show that color preferences correlate with self-concept and emotional needs. Black vehicles signal sophistication and power—customers choosing black often use words like "professional," "serious," and "commanding." White represents modernity and simplicity, appealing to buyers who value clean aesthetics and practicality. Red conveys energy and confidence, attracting customers who want to project boldness.

The ethical application isn't manipulating color choices but recognizing what customers reveal through their preferences. When someone gravitates toward a particular color despite practical considerations, they're showing you something about their identity. Ask questions that explore this: "What draws you to that color?" Often, customers will share insights—"I've always seen myself in a red car" or "Black feels more executive"—that reveal deeper motivations you can address authentically.

I've found that customers who initially request "practical" colors like silver or grey but keep glancing at bolder options are often negotiating between their responsible self and their aspirational self. Your role isn't pushing them toward higher-margin colors but helping them feel confident choosing what genuinely resonates. "A lot of customers start with practical colors but end up choosing what makes them feel good every time they see the vehicle. What would make you excited to walk out to your car each morning?"

Status Signaling and Social Identity

Research in social psychology demonstrates that possessions—particularly visible ones like vehicles—communicate social identity and status. Luxury brands like Mercedes-Benz and BMW carry associations with success and achievement. Performance vehicles signal ambition and individuality. Eco-friendly options like Tesla reflect values around innovation and environmental responsibility.

The key insight: customers aren't being shallow when status matters to them—they're responding to legitimate psychological needs for social belonging and self-esteem. The executive considering a luxury sedan isn't just buying transportation; they're investing in a tool that signals credibility to clients and peers. The parent choosing a premium SUV is often expressing their commitment to family protection and providing the best for their children.

Your ethical approach acknowledges these motivations without judgment. When customers mention what colleagues drive or express concern about how a vehicle will be perceived, they're trusting you with genuine concerns. Validate rather than dismiss: "Image matters in your profession—that makes complete sense. Let's find something that projects the right message while meeting your practical needs."

Lifestyle Alignment and Aspiration

Vehicles often represent not just current identity but aspirational self-concept—who customers want to become. The urban professional buying a rugged SUV may be expressing their desire for adventure and outdoor experiences, even if their current lifestyle is mostly city-based. The family purchasing a sportier vehicle than strictly necessary might be maintaining connection to their pre-parent identity.

Understanding this helps you position vehicles as enablers of desired lifestyle rather than just meeting current needs. During test drives, ask customers to envision themselves using the vehicle: "Picture yourself pulling up to your office in this—how does that feel?" or "Imagine taking your family on that road trip you've been planning." These questions help customers emotionally connect with how the vehicle fits their identity and aspirations.

The ethical power of understanding color, status, and identity psychology is that you're genuinely helping customers choose vehicles they'll love long-term—not just today, but months and years later when they're deciding whether to refer friends or return for their next purchase. When customers feel their vehicle authentically reflects who they are, satisfaction deepens beyond features and financing into something more meaningful: the confidence that their choice was right for them.

Reading Unspoken Signals: Body Language, Questions, and Behavioral Cues That Reveal True Priorities

I'll never forget the Saturday afternoon when a couple walked into our dealership, and everything they *said* told me they were just browsing—but everything they *showed* me screamed that they were ready to buy today. "We're just looking," the husband announced as they entered. "We're not buying anything for at least three months." His wife nodded in agreement. But I noticed something: they'd walked directly past eight other vehicles to stand in front of a specific SUV. The wife's hand was already on the door handle. They exchanged a quick glance—the kind of wordless communication that happens between people who've made decisions together for years. Their body language was telling a completely different story than their words.

That experience, early in my career, taught me something crucial: customers often don't—or can't—articulate their true priorities directly. Sometimes they're protecting themselves from sales pressure. Sometimes they haven't consciously recognized what matters most to them. And sometimes they're negotiating between competing priorities they haven't resolved yet. Your ability to read these unspoken signals—body language, question patterns, and behavioral cues—determines whether you can genuinely help customers or simply respond to what they think they should want.

The Body Language Baseline: What Normal Looks Like

The first skill is establishing each customer's baseline behavior when they arrive, then noticing changes as the interaction progresses. Some people naturally make limited eye contact or stand with crossed arms—that's their comfortable default, not a sign of resistance. But when someone who's been open and engaged suddenly crosses their arms or steps back, that shift signals something worth exploring.

Watch for clusters of signals rather than isolated gestures. A customer who leans forward, maintains eye contact, asks detailed questions, and touches the vehicle is showing genuine interest regardless of their verbal hesitations. Conversely, someone who says all the right words but keeps glancing at their phone, maintains physical distance, and offers only brief answers is signaling disengagement.

During test drives, observe what captures attention. The customer who adjusts the seat multiple times, tests every control, and comments on visibility is mentally taking ownership. The one who drives mechanically without exploring features hasn't emotionally connected yet. I learned to extend test drives when I noticed ownership behaviors emerging—"Would you like to try the highway entrance to feel the acceleration?"—giving that emotional connection time to solidify.

Questions Reveal Hidden Priorities

The questions customers ask—and how persistently they return to certain topics—reveal what truly matters beneath their stated criteria. A customer who repeatedly circles back to safety features despite claiming fuel economy is their priority is showing you their real concern. Someone who asks detailed questions about warranty coverage and service intervals is revealing anxiety about reliability or past negative experiences.

Pay attention to *whose* questions dominate when couples or families shop together. The person asking most questions often holds decision-making authority, but not always—sometimes the quieter individual is processing carefully and will ultimately determine the outcome. I learned to address both partners equally and watch for subtle approval signals: the nod, the slight smile, the glance that says "I like this one."

Behavioral Cues That Predict Outcomes

Time investment is one of the most reliable behavioral indicators. Customers who return for second visits, bring family members for input, or spend extended time exploring features are signaling serious intent even if they verbally express uncertainty. The customer who says "we're just starting to look" but has already test-driven three vehicles and researched financing options online is much further along than their words suggest.

Digital behavior provides valuable context before customers ever arrive.[13] When someone fills out detailed online inquiry forms, engages in extended chat conversations, or requests specific vehicle information, they're demonstrating investment that predicts in-person seriousness. I started reviewing customers' digital interactions before meeting them, which helped me understand their priorities and concerns from the first moment.

The Ethical Application: Helping Rather Than Manipulating

Understanding unspoken signals isn't about exploiting vulnerabilities—it's about recognizing what customers need even when they can't articulate it clearly. When that couple stood in front of the SUV claiming they weren't ready to buy, I didn't pressure them. Instead, I acknowledged their timeline while addressing what their behavior revealed: "I hear you're planning for three months out—that's smart. Since you're here, would it be helpful to test drive this model so you know how it compares as you continue researching?" They drove it, loved it, and bought it that day—not because I pressured them, but because I recognized they were further along than they realized and simply needed permission to act on what they already wanted.

Reading unspoken signals transforms you from someone who responds to stated needs into someone who understands actual needs—the foundation of consultative selling that builds trust, generates referrals, and creates customers who return because you genuinely helped them.[16] [13]Understanding customer psychology isn't an optional skill for modern automotive sales professionals—it's the foundation that everything else builds upon. Throughout this chapter, we've explored how purchase decisions happen on multiple levels simultaneously, with emotional drivers leading the way while rational justifications follow behind to validate what the heart has already chosen. We've examined how fundamental human needs—from safety and belonging to esteem and self-actualization—shape what customers truly seek when they walk onto your showroom floor. And we've discovered how cognitive biases, identity expression, and unspoken signals reveal priorities that customers themselves may not consciously recognize.

The practical power of this psychological understanding becomes clear when you consider what separates successful consultative sales professionals from those who struggle despite knowing every vehicle specification and financing option. The difference isn't product knowledge—it's the ability to recognize that the anxious parent asking endless safety questions is trying to protect their child, that the executive drawn to a luxury brand is fulfilling legitimate esteem needs, that the customer who says "I need to think about it" is often experiencing disconnect between emotional attraction and rational confidence. When you develop this recognition, your entire approach shifts from convincing to collaborating, from selling to serving.

What makes this psychological insight ethically powerful is that you're not manipulating customers—you're genuinely helping them understand their own decision-making process and feel confident about choices that align with their actual needs and values. The customer who recognizes that their vehicle choice reflects their identity and aspirations makes decisions they'll feel good about years later, generating the referrals and repeat business that build sustainable careers. The sales professional who can read unspoken signals and address underlying concerns creates trust that transcends individual transactions.

As you move forward into the next chapters, where we'll explore specific techniques for building rapport, handling objections, and closing deals, remember that every strategy and tactic we discuss rests on this psychological foundation. The rapport-building techniques in Chapter 3 work because they address customers' need for trust and genuine connection. The objection-handling frameworks we'll examine succeed because they recognize that resistance reveals unmet needs rather than obstacles to overcome. The closing strategies that generate long-term satisfaction honor both the emotional drivers and rational justifications that customers require to feel confident.

The automotive sales landscape has evolved dramatically from the high-pressure tactics of previous decades, and customer psychology explains why. Today's digitally-informed buyers arrive with extensive research and infinite options—they don't need you to provide information they can find online. What they need is someone who understands the human dimensions of their decision: the anxiety beneath their questions, the identity concerns driving their preferences, the cognitive biases shaping their perceptions, and the unspoken priorities their behavior reveals. Master this psychological understanding, and you'll discover that modern automotive sales success isn't about overcoming customer resistance—it's about recognizing what customers truly need and genuinely helping them achieve it. That's the foundation of relationship-driven selling that doesn't just close deals today but builds careers that thrive for decades.

Chapter 3

Car Buyer Rapport Building: Establishing Genuine Trust in a Skeptical Market

Trust doesn't announce itself with a handshake and a smile—it accumulates through dozens of micro-interactions where your words align with your actions and your interest in the customer proves genuine rather than transactional. In an industry where skepticism has become the customer's default defense mechanism, the sales professional who can authentically demonstrate trustworthiness gains an advantage more powerful than any pricing strategy or product knowledge. Trust doesn't announce itself with a handshake and a smile—it accumulates through dozens of micro-interactions where your words align with your actions and your interest in the customer proves genuine rather than transactional. In an industry where skepticism has become the customer's default defense mechanism, the sales professional who can authentically demonstrate trustworthiness gains an advantage more powerful than any pricing strategy or product knowledge.

This chapter addresses the most fundamental challenge you'll face in automotive sales: customers walk through your door expecting to be manipulated. They've heard the stories, read the warnings, and armed themselves with research specifically to defend against tactics they assume you'll deploy. This skepticism isn't personal—it's the accumulated weight of decades of industry reputation, reinforced by every negative experience they've heard about from friends, family, or online reviews. Your task isn't to overcome this skepticism through clever techniques or disarming charm. It's to systematically demonstrate, through specific behaviors and communication patterns, that you're genuinely different from what they expect.

The rapport-building strategies in this chapter aren't superficial tricks for "getting customers to like you." They're foundational practices for establishing the authentic trust that today's informed buyers require before they'll seriously consider your guidance. You'll learn how to navigate those critical opening minutes when customers are most guarded, how to use active listening as a trust-building tool rather than just a sales technique, and how to demonstrate transparency in ways that differentiate you from competitors still operating with information asymmetry. Most importantly, you'll discover how to maintain rapport beyond the sale— transforming one-time customers into long-term relationships that generate the referrals and repeat business that define sustainable success.

The digital age has made rapport building simultaneously more challenging and more valuable. Customers arrive with extensive research, competitive quotes, and online reviews that have already shaped their expectations. They've likely read about common sales tactics and primed themselves to resist. But this same digital connectivity creates opportunities: the sales professional who builds genuine trust doesn't just earn a customer—they earn an advocate whose online reviews, social media mentions, and personal recommendations reach hundreds of potential future customers. In a market where reputation travels instantly and authentically, your ability to build real rapport becomes your most powerful competitive advantage.

Throughout this chapter, you'll follow real dealership scenarios that illustrate how trust either develops or deteriorates based on specific choices sales professionals make. You'll see how acknowledging customer skepticism honestly can paradoxically reduce it, how transparency about limitations builds more credibility than false promises, and how follow-through on small commitments creates the foundation for major purchase decisions. By the end, you'll have practical frameworks you can implement immediately—not scripts to memorize, but principles to guide authentic interactions that honor customer intelligence while demonstrating that you're genuinely invested in their satisfaction beyond your commission.

The Trust Deficit: Understanding Why Car Buyers Arrive Skeptical and How to Acknowledge It Honestly

I remember the exact moment I understood the depth of customer skepticism in automotive sales. A woman named Rachel walked onto our lot, and before I could finish introducing myself, she held up her hand and said, "I've already been to three dealerships today. I know all the tricks. Just show me the invoice price and we'll talk." Her tone wasn't hostile—it was weary. She'd armored herself for battle before even giving me a chance to prove I might be different.

Rachel's defensive posture wasn't personal, and it wasn't irrational. The automotive industry consistently ranks among the least trusted consumer sectors[24], with research showing that 76% of buyers don't trust dealerships to be honest about pricing[27]. When 86% of car buyers worry about hidden fees[27] and nearly a third have walked away from a dealership specifically due to honesty concerns[27], skepticism becomes the logical default position. Your customers arrive expecting manipulation because the industry has, collectively, taught them to expect it.

The trust deficit runs deeper than pricing concerns. A 2024 survey revealed that 37% of buyers have abandoned a dealership purchase out of uncertainty about the seller's honesty, and over a quarter discovered serious mechanical issues within six months—often costing thousands of dollars[25]. More troubling still, over 15% of sellers admit to hiding known problems from buyers[25]. These aren't abstract statistics; they're your customers' lived experiences and the stories they've heard from friends and family.

The generational dimension of this trust crisis matters tremendously for your career longevity. While baby boomers maintain moderate trust in dealerships, that trust drops significantly among Generation X and millennials, reaching its lowest point with Generation Z[24]. These younger buyers, raised on transparent e-commerce platforms like Amazon where pricing is clear and reviews are readily available, find traditional dealership opacity particularly jarring[24]. As these demographics become your primary customer base, the trust deficit will only widen unless you actively address it.

Here's what most sales training gets wrong: they teach you to *overcome* skepticism through rapport-building techniques designed to lower customer defenses. But skepticism isn't an obstacle to bypass—it's legitimate self-protection based on rational assessment of industry behavior. The most powerful response isn't to deflect or minimize it, but to acknowledge it directly and honestly.

When Rachel told me she knew "all the tricks," I made a choice that felt risky but proved transformative. I said, "You're right to be cautious. This industry has earned its reputation, and I can't change what you've experienced at other dealerships. What I can do is show you exactly how we price vehicles, explain every fee before we get to paperwork, and give you my personal cell number so you can reach me if any issues come up after the sale. And if at any point I do something that feels like one of those tricks, call me on it."

Rachel's shoulders visibly relaxed. By acknowledging the elephant in the room—the industry's trust problem—I'd done something none of the previous three dealerships had done: I'd validated her experience rather than asking her to pretend it didn't exist.

The data supports this approach. Buyers who perceive transparency in the sales process are nearly three times more likely to trust their dealer[28]. But here's the critical insight: 94% of dealers recognize a significant gap between what they consider transparent and what customers consider transparent[26]. You might think you're being open while your customer still feels information is being withheld.

Acknowledging the trust deficit honestly means naming it explicitly in your early conversations. When customers arrive with competitive quotes, research printouts, or defensive body language, try saying something like: "I know car buying has a reputation for being stressful and sometimes dishonest. That's not how I do business, but I understand you have no reason to believe that yet. How about we take this at whatever pace feels comfortable, and if anything doesn't feel right, you tell me?" This simple acknowledgment transforms the dynamic from adversarial to collaborative.

The trust deficit isn't your fault personally, but rebuilding trust is your professional responsibility. Every transparent conversation, every fee explained proactively, every promise kept after the sale—these are deposits in an account that benefits not just your career but the industry's future credibility.

First Impressions That Build Rather Than Break Trust: The Critical Opening Minutes

I learned about the power of first impressions the hard way. Early in my career, I watched a colleague lose a sale in the first ninety seconds without realizing it. A couple walked onto the lot, and before they'd taken five steps, he approached with an enthusiastic "So, are we buying a car today?" The woman's face tightened immediately. Her husband's posture shifted from open to defensive. They stayed for politeness, test-drove a vehicle, but I could see they'd already decided they wouldn't buy from someone who'd treated them like a transaction before learning their names.

Research confirms what that painful moment taught me: customers form lasting judgments about salespeople within the first 30 seconds to three minutes of interaction.[29][33] These snap assessments, shaped by tone, body language, and initial words, are remarkably difficult to reverse. In an industry where 76% of buyers already distrust dealerships to be honest about pricing, those opening minutes carry enormous weight.[30][32] You're not starting from neutral ground—you're starting from skepticism, and your first words and actions either confirm or challenge that preconception.

The greeting sets everything in motion. A warm, genuine welcome—"Hi, thanks for coming in today. I'm Sarah"—signals respect and openness. Contrast that with transactional openers that immediately trigger defenses: "What can I put you in today?" or "Are you ready to make a deal?" These phrases, however well-intentioned, communicate that you see a commission rather than a person.[29] Your customer's internal walls go up instantly.

Body language speaks before you do. Approach with open posture, genuine smile, and comfortable eye contact that respects cultural and individual differences.[29][33] Stand at a respectful distance—close enough to be engaged, far enough to avoid invading personal space. If customers are browsing and seem to want space, acknowledge them warmly but give them room: "Welcome! I'm here if you have any questions." This respects their autonomy while making yourself available.

The most powerful trust-building tool in those opening minutes is the open-ended question focused on understanding rather than selling.[29][31] Instead of "What's your budget?" try "What brings you in today?" or "Tell me about what you're looking for in your next vehicle." These questions invite conversation rather than interrogation. They signal that you're genuinely interested in their needs, not just qualifying them as prospects.

Personalization transforms generic interactions into human connections. Use customers' names as soon as you learn them—it creates immediate belonging and recognition.[31] If they mention they've been researching online, acknowledge that effort: "I'm glad you've done your homework—that makes my job easier because we can focus on what matters most to you."[29] This validates their preparation rather than seeing it as a threat to your expertise.

Transparency from the first moment builds credibility that pays dividends throughout the process. Research from the University of Denver found that salespeople who revealed invoice pricing early in negotiations significantly increased buyer trust, which later translated to greater willingness to consider additional products and services.[32] Hiding information that customers can easily verify online doesn't protect your position—it destroys trust before you've had a chance to earn it.[30][32]

Match your energy to theirs. If customers arrive energetic and enthusiastic, respond in kind. If they seem reserved or cautious, use a softer, more measured approach.[29] This subtle mirroring—adapting your pace and tone to theirs—creates subconscious rapport that makes people feel understood and comfortable.

What you avoid matters as much as what you do. Never jump immediately into product features, dealership awards, or technical specifications that don't relate to what the customer has expressed.[29] Don't create artificial urgency with phrases like "This deal ends today" or "Someone else is looking at this vehicle."[29] These pressure tactics might occasionally force a quick decision, but they poison the relationship and virtually guarantee you'll never see that customer again or receive a referral.

Those critical opening minutes aren't about demonstrating your sales skills—they're about demonstrating your humanity, respect, and genuine interest in helping someone make a decision they'll feel good about long after the excitement of a new vehicle fades.[29][30][31][32]

Active Listening as a Trust-Building Tool: Techniques for Demonstrating Genuine Interest

I learned the true power of active listening during my third year on the showroom floor, when a customer named Marcus taught me that hearing and listening are fundamentally different skills. He'd been speaking for nearly five minutes about his family's needs—his daughter's soccer schedule, his wife's commute, weekend camping trips—when I interrupted to highlight a vehicle's cargo capacity. Marcus stopped mid-sentence, gave me a look I'll never forget, and said quietly, "You're not actually listening to me, are you? You're just waiting for your turn to talk." He was right, and he walked out. That moment cost me a sale, but it taught me a lesson worth far more.

Active listening isn't a passive activity where you simply stay quiet while customers speak. It's an engaged, intentional practice that demonstrates genuine interest through specific behaviors customers can recognize and respond to. Research consistently shows that customers are more likely to trust and purchase from sales professionals who actively listen and respond to their specific circumstances[34][35][36][37][38], with top-performing salespeople employing these techniques as a cornerstone of their success[38].

The foundation of active listening starts with open-ended questions that invite detailed responses. Instead of asking "What's your budget?"—which triggers defensiveness—try "What features are most important to you in your next vehicle?" or "How will you be using this car day-to-day?"[34][39] These questions signal that you're genuinely interested in understanding their situation, not just qualifying them as a prospect. When a customer mentions they have a growing family, follow up with "Tell me more about what that means for your vehicle needs" rather than immediately jumping to minivan recommendations.

Paraphrasing what customers say proves you're processing their words, not just hearing them. When someone explains they need reliability because their current car left them stranded twice, respond with "So dependability is your top priority—you want confidence that this vehicle won't let you down. Is that right?"[34][37] This simple technique, supported by sales training research, validates their concern and creates space for them to clarify or expand. I use this constantly, and customers visibly relax when they realize I'm actually tracking their priorities.

Non-verbal engagement amplifies your verbal attention. Maintain comfortable eye contact without staring.[37] Lean in slightly when customers share important details. Nod affirmatively to show you're following their thoughts. Keep your body language open—arms uncrossed, posture oriented toward them.[37] These physical cues communicate respect and interest more powerfully than any words. Equally important: silence your phone, close your laptop if you're taking notes digitally, and eliminate distractions. When a customer sees you've given them your complete attention, trust begins building immediately.

The most common active listening failure is interrupting.[37] When customers pause, resist the urge to fill the silence with product features or solutions. Give them space to gather their thoughts and continue. Some of my most valuable insights have come from simply waiting three seconds longer than felt comfortable—customers often share their real concerns in those moments of silence.

Affirmations validate customer feelings and build rapport authentically.[34] When someone mentions they're nervous about the purchase because it's their first new car, acknowledge that: "That's completely understandable— this is a significant decision, and I appreciate you sharing that with me. Let's make sure you feel completely confident before moving forward."

This simple validation transforms the dynamic from transactional to collaborative.

Follow-up questions demonstrate depth of interest. If a customer mentions their previous vehicle had reliability issues, ask "What specifically went wrong?" or "How did the dealership handle those problems?"[36] These questions uncover not just practical needs but emotional drivers—perhaps they're not just seeking reliability, but also reassurance that you'll support them if issues arise.

Active listening streamlines your entire sales process.[34][37] When customers feel genuinely heard, objections decrease because you've already addressed their real concerns.[37] Your recommendations land with more impact because they're clearly connected to what customers told you matters most. And the trust you build through listening creates loyal customers who return and refer others[37][38]—the foundation of sustainable success in modern automotive sales.

Transparency and Honesty: When and How to Admit What You Don't Know or Can't Do

I'll never forget the moment I realized that admitting ignorance could be more powerful than faking expertise. A customer named David asked me a highly technical question about the hybrid system's regenerative braking calibration in a vehicle I'd only started selling the previous week. My instinct—honed by years of feeling like I needed to have every answer—was to improvise something that sounded plausible. Instead, I took a breath and said, "That's a great question, and I want to give you accurate information rather than guessing. Let me get our product specialist who can explain exactly how that system works." David's entire demeanor shifted. "Thank you for being honest," he said. "The last dealership I visited made up an answer, and I knew it was wrong. That's why I left."

That interaction taught me what research has consistently confirmed: transparency builds trust, and trust sells cars more effectively than any amount of manufactured expertise.[42] In an industry where 76% of buyers don't trust dealerships to be honest about pricing, your willingness to admit what you don't know becomes a powerful differentiator. When you acknowledge limitations honestly, you signal authenticity—and authenticity is the foundation of the relationship-driven selling that defines modern automotive success.[42 45]

The strategic power of admission lies in what it communicates about your priorities. When you say "I don't know, but I'll find out," you're telling customers that accuracy matters more to you than appearing knowledgeable. When you admit "I can't get you that price," you're demonstrating that you won't make promises you can't keep. These moments of vulnerability create credibility that no amount of smooth talking can replicate.[42 45]

The key is pairing admission with commitment to resolution. Never leave customers hanging with "I don't know" as a complete sentence. Instead, structure your response in three parts: acknowledge the gap honestly, commit to finding the answer, and provide a specific timeline. "I want to make sure you get accurate information about that warranty coverage. Let me check with our finance manager and call you back within the hour with the exact details." This approach transforms a potential weakness into a demonstration of customer-focused service.

Know the boundaries of what you can and cannot promise. If a customer asks whether you can match a competitor's price that's below your dealership's cost, don't create false hope. Say clearly: "I appreciate you sharing that quote. I can't match that specific number because it's below what we paid for the vehicle, but let me show you our pricing breakdown and explain what we include that might not be reflected in that quote." This transparency prevents the disappointment and resentment that come from discovering limitations late in the negotiation process.[43] [44] [46]

Technical questions you can't answer immediately are opportunities to demonstrate your network and resources. When customers ask about specifications beyond your current knowledge, connect them with your service department, product specialists, or manufacturer resources. "I want you to have complete confidence in this information. Our service manager has twenty years of experience with this engine—let me get him on the phone so he can walk you through exactly how the maintenance schedule works." This approach shows customers they're buying from a dealership with depth of expertise, not just from you individually.

Digital transparency extends these principles to your online presence.[40] [42] When customers email questions you can't answer immediately, respond promptly acknowledging receipt and providing a timeline for the complete answer rather than leaving them wondering if you received their message. If your dealership's website lacks information customers are seeking, admit that gap and offer to provide the details directly: "Great question—that specification isn't listed on our site yet, but I'll send you the complete breakdown this afternoon."

The admission that generates the most anxiety for salespeople is "I can't do that" in response to customer requests—whether about pricing, delivery timing, or special accommodations. But customers respect clear boundaries far more than vague promises that later prove impossible. When you must decline a request, explain why honestly and offer alternatives: "I can't have the vehicle ready by Friday because our detail department is backed up, but I can have it ready Monday morning and deliver it to your home so you don't have to make the trip back here."[45]

This transparency doesn't mean volunteering every limitation unprompted or undermining your own capabilities. It means responding honestly when gaps in knowledge or ability surface, and proactively addressing limitations that will directly impact the customer's experience.[47] The sales professionals who master this balance discover something powerful: customers don't expect perfection—they expect honesty. When you deliver that consistently, you build the trust that transforms skeptical shoppers into loyal advocates who return for their next vehicle and refer everyone they know.[40 41 44]

Building Long-Term Rapport: Follow-Up Strategies That Prove Your Interest Extends Beyond the Sale

The sale isn't the finish line—it's the starting point of a relationship that will either fade into forgotten transactions or grow into the referral-generating, repeat-business foundation of your career. I learned this lesson painfully in my second year on the showroom floor when I ran into a customer named Linda at a grocery store six months after she'd purchased a vehicle from me. She looked right past me, no recognition in her eyes, because I'd disappeared from her life the moment she drove off the lot. That awkward non-encounter taught me something crucial: customers don't forget salespeople who vanish after the sale—they just never think of them again when it's time for their next purchase or when friends ask for recommendations.

The follow-up strategies that build long-term rapport aren't about pestering customers with thinly-veiled sales pitches disguised as "checking in." They're systematic touchpoints that deliver genuine value, demonstrate ongoing care, and keep you present in customers' lives without being intrusive.[48 50 51] Research shows that dealerships prioritizing post-sale engagement consistently outperform those treating transactions as endpoints, with AI-driven customer engagement strategies increasing revenue by 15% through personalized, timely follow-up.[49] But technology only amplifies what should already be authentic—your genuine interest in customer satisfaction beyond your commission.

The first touchpoint happens within 24 hours of delivery.[52] Send a personalized thank-you message—email, text, or handwritten note depending on what feels natural for your relationship with that customer.[48 50 52] Reference something specific from your conversations: "I hope you're enjoying the new Outback, and that it's everything you needed for those weekend camping trips you mentioned." This specificity proves you were actually listening, not just processing a transaction.[50] Within the first week, make a brief call asking if they have questions about features or need help with anything. This isn't a sales call—it's genuine support during the adjustment period when new owners are most likely to feel overwhelmed by unfamiliar technology.

Map your follow-up calendar around natural ownership milestones.[48] A 30-day satisfaction check addresses any early concerns before they become problems. Six-month service reminders demonstrate you're thinking about their vehicle's long-term health. One-year anniversary messages reinforce the relationship. For lease customers, proactive communication 90 days before lease-end positions you as their trusted advisor for the next vehicle decision rather than forcing them to start the shopping process from scratch with strangers.

Personalization transforms generic follow-up into relationship maintenance.[50 52] When you send maintenance tips, make them specific to the vehicle they purchased and how they use it.[50 52] If a customer mentioned they have a long highway commute, share information about optimal tire pressure for fuel efficiency on extended drives. If they bought for family road trips, send seasonal safety reminders before holiday travel periods. This targeted value delivery keeps you relevant without being salesy.[51]

Multi-channel communication respects different customer preferences.[49][51][52] Some people prefer text messages, others email, some appreciate occasional phone calls. Pay attention to how customers respond and adapt accordingly. Use your CRM system to track these preferences and interaction history—technology should enable personalization, not replace the human judgment about when and how to reach out.[49]

The most powerful follow-up strategy is addressing issues proactively and transparently.[50] When customers contact you with problems—and they will—your response defines whether this becomes a relationship-ending disappointment or a trust-building demonstration of your commitment. Acknowledge concerns immediately, explain the resolution process clearly, and follow up after the issue is resolved to confirm satisfaction.[50] Customers who experience problems that get handled well often become more loyal than those who never had issues, because you've proven your support extends beyond the sale.

Build systematic referral generation into your follow-up process, but earn it first.[50] After several months of demonstrated care and successful ownership experience, it's entirely appropriate to say, "I'm glad everything's working out well with your vehicle. If you know anyone else who might benefit from the same kind of straightforward, supportive experience we've had together, I'd appreciate you sharing my contact information." This request feels natural rather than presumptuous because you've already proven your value through consistent follow-through.

The sales professionals who master long-term rapport building discover something remarkable: their job gets progressively easier over time. While colleagues constantly chase new prospects, you're receiving calls from previous customers ready for their next vehicle, referrals from satisfied buyers, and the compounding benefits of a reputation built on relationships that extend far beyond individual transactions.[48] [49] [50] [51] [52]Building genuine rapport in automotive sales isn't a technique you deploy—it's a commitment you make to treating every customer as an intelligent person deserving of respect, honesty, and patience. The strategies in this chapter work not because they're clever tactics that bypass customer defenses, but because they're authentic behaviors that honor the legitimate skepticism customers bring to the dealership. When you acknowledge the trust deficit honestly, make strong first impressions through genuine interest rather than sales enthusiasm, listen actively to what customers actually need, admit what you don't know, and maintain relationships beyond the sale, you're not just building rapport—you're differentiating yourself in a market where authenticity has become the scarcest and most valuable commodity.

The transformation from skeptical stranger to trusting customer doesn't happen through a single perfect interaction. It accumulates through dozens of small moments where your actions align with your words: when you turn your computer screen toward customers to show them exactly what you're looking at, when you acknowledge a competitor's legitimate advantage rather than dismissing it, when you call back within the timeframe you promised, when you respond to a text question three months after the sale with the same attentiveness you showed during the purchase process. These micro-interactions create the foundation of trust that not only closes sales but generates the referrals and repeat business that define sustainable success in modern automotive retail.

The digital dimension of rapport building amplifies everything—both positive and negative. A single authentic interaction can become a five-star review that reaches hundreds of potential customers. A moment of dishonesty or pressure can become a one-star warning that costs you dozens of future opportunities. Your reputation is no longer confined to the customers you personally interact with—it extends to everyone they're connected to online and everyone who reads their reviews. This reality makes relationship-focused selling not just ethically superior but commercially essential. The sales professionals who understand this don't view transparency and honesty as constraints on their effectiveness—they recognize them as their most powerful competitive advantages.

The rapport-building approach detailed in this chapter requires patience that some of your colleagues may question. You'll encounter customers who don't buy immediately, managers who pressure you to close harder, and moments when high-pressure tactics might generate a quick sale. But the long-term mathematics are undeniable: customers who trust you return for their next vehicle, send referrals without being asked, leave positive reviews that attract new prospects, and create a compounding business model where your career gets progressively easier rather than requiring constant prospecting. The initial investment of time and authenticity pays dividends that extend far beyond individual transactions.

As you move forward in your automotive sales career, remember that every customer interaction is an opportunity to either confirm or challenge the industry's reputation. When you choose transparency over manipulation, patience over pressure, and genuine interest over transactional efficiency, you're not just building your own success—you're contributing to the evolution of an entire profession. The customers who walk into your dealership expecting to be manipulated and walk out feeling respected and supported become the most powerful marketing force you'll ever have. That's the real power of authentic rapport building: it transforms skeptics into advocates, transactions into relationships, and sales careers into sustainable businesses built on trust, reputation, and the kind of customer loyalty that no amount of advertising can purchase.

Chapter 4

Modern Car Selling Techniques: Adapting to the Digitally-Informed Customer

Florence had been selling cars for fifteen years when she encountered a customer who made her question everything she thought she knew about her profession. The young man walked onto the lot with his smartphone in hand, and before she could finish her greeting, he said, "I know exactly which vehicle I want, I know what you paid for it, and I know what three other dealerships are willing to sell it for." Florence had been selling cars for fifteen years when she encountered a customer who made her question everything she thought she knew about her profession. The young man walked onto the lot with his smartphone in hand, and before she could finish her greeting, he said, "I know exactly which vehicle I want, I know what you paid for it, and I know what three other dealerships are willing to sell it for."

If you've been in automotive sales for any length of time, you've experienced some version of this moment—the customer who arrives armed with research that would have taken weeks to compile just a decade ago, now accessible in an afternoon of browsing. The digitally-informed buyer represents the most significant shift in automotive sales since the industry's inception, fundamentally transforming what customers need from sales professionals and rendering obsolete the information-gatekeeping approach that once defined dealership success.

This chapter addresses the reality that today's car buyers complete sixty to seventy percent of their purchase journey online before ever contacting a dealership. They've compared specifications across multiple websites, watched video reviews from sources they trust more than salespeople, calculated payments using online tools, checked invoice pricing on consumer sites, and solicited quotes via email from every dealership within driving distance. They arrive at your showroom not lacking information, but drowning in it—and that distinction changes everything about your role in their journey.

The sales professionals who thrive with digitally-informed customers understand a crucial truth: the internet didn't eliminate the need for automotive salespeople—it elevated what customers need from them. When information was scarce, your value came from knowing more than the customer. Now that information is abundant, your value comes from helping customers translate data into confidence, validating their research against real-world experience, answering questions that websites can't address, and providing the human reassurance that algorithms cannot replicate.

Throughout this chapter, you'll learn specific techniques for engaging customers who've already completed extensive online research. You'll discover how to respond to digital inquiries—via email, text, and chat—in ways that convert online interest into showroom visits and build trust before you ever meet face-to-face. You'll master strategies for adding value beyond information, positioning yourself as a trusted advisor rather than competing with the internet as an information source. You'll explore how to leverage technology on the showroom floor as a collaborative tool that enhances rather than replaces human connection. And you'll learn frameworks for bridging the gap between online research and in-person experience, guiding customers from information overload to purchase confidence.

The approaches in this chapter aren't theoretical—they're proven techniques from salespeople who've successfully adapted to the digital transformation, building sustainable careers by working with rather than against how modern customers research and buy vehicles. Whether you're a career changer encountering your first digitally-informed buyer or a veteran adapting to customers who know your invoice pricing before introducing themselves, these strategies will help you discover your irreplaceable value in an information-rich marketplace.

The Digitally-Informed Customer Profile: Understanding How Online Research Changes the Sales Dynamic

Understanding who walks through your dealership doors today requires recognizing a fundamental truth: the customer sitting across from you has likely invested more time researching their potential purchase than you spent preparing for the conversation. According to Cox Automotive research, ninety-five percent of car shoppers now use online resources before contacting a dealership[54][53][56], spending an average of fourteen hours across multiple websites[54] gathering information that once existed exclusively in the minds of sales professionals.

This isn't your father's car buyer—and that's not a cliché, it's a measurable demographic shift. When I started in automotive sales two decades ago, customers arrived seeking information. Today, they arrive seeking validation, clarification, and confidence in decisions they've already substantially researched. The digitally-informed customer knows your invoice pricing before introducing themselves, has compared your inventory to three competitors, watched video reviews from sources they trust more than salespeople, and calculated monthly payments using online tools more sophisticated than what many dealerships provide their staff.

The research patterns reveal how thoroughly the landscape has shifted. Modern buyers visit an average of 4.2 websites during their research process[54], with seventy-six percent running online searches before buying and thirty-three percent of that research happening on mobile devices[54]. They're comparing specifications across manufacturer sites, reading owner reviews on automotive forums, checking reliability ratings on consumer publications, and soliciting email quotes from every dealership within fifty miles. By the time they contact you, they've completed sixty to seventy percent of their purchase journey without ever speaking to a sales professional.

This creates what I call the "information paradox"—customers arrive both highly informed and completely overwhelmed. They know the horsepower, fuel economy, and safety ratings, but they're uncertain whether that data translates to the right choice for their specific situation. They've read conflicting reviews and don't know which to trust. They understand the numbers but question whether they're making a sound financial decision. They've researched everything yet still need something only you can provide: human guidance through complexity.

The generational dimension matters significantly. Younger buyers, particularly Gen Z and Millennials, embrace digital research even more thoroughly than older demographics. Salesforce research found that thirty-four percent of Gen Z buyers are willing to purchase vehicles entirely online, compared to just nineteen percent of buyers over forty-five[53][55]. These younger customers increasingly trust AI-powered tools for recommendations and maintenance scheduling[55], with seventy-nine percent of Gen Z wanting AI agents to recommend vehicles based on their preferences[55].

What does this mean for your daily work? The traditional sales approach—where you controlled information flow and guided customers through a linear discovery process—no longer applies. Digitally-informed customers don't need you to recite specifications they've already memorized or explain features they've watched demonstrated in YouTube videos. They need you to translate their research into real-world context, validate their conclusions against your experience with hundreds of similar buyers, address concerns that websites can't answer, and provide the confidence that comes from working with someone who genuinely understands their situation.

The sales dynamic has fundamentally inverted. You're no longer the primary information source—you're the translator, validator, and confidence-builder. The customer isn't coming to learn about vehicles; they're coming to confirm they've learned correctly and to experience what research alone cannot provide: the feel of the vehicle, the trustworthiness of the dealership relationship, and the assurance that their significant investment is sound. Understanding this shift isn't just helpful—it's essential to remaining relevant in a marketplace where forty-two percent of buyers will switch brands if their online experience fails to meet expectations[53].

Your value hasn't diminished in the digital age—it's evolved. The question isn't whether customers need you, but whether you've adapted to provide what they actually need now rather than what they needed twenty years ago.

Responding to Online Inquiries: Email, Text, and Chat Strategies That Convert Digital Interest Into Showroom Visits

The moment a customer submits an online inquiry—whether through your dealership website, a third-party platform, or social media—a clock starts ticking. Research from automotive industry studies shows that responding within ten minutes increases your likelihood of meaningful engagement exponentially compared to waiting even an hour.[17] Yet I've watched countless dealerships treat digital inquiries as tomorrow's problem, sending generic responses hours later while wondering why customers have already visited competitors.

I learned this lesson painfully during my second year in automotive sales. A customer named Rachel submitted a detailed inquiry through our website on a Wednesday afternoon, asking specific questions about a crossover SUV she'd researched extensively. I was with another customer and figured I'd respond when I finished—about ninety minutes later. My carefully crafted reply went unanswered. Three days later, Rachel purchased the identical vehicle from a dealership forty minutes farther from her home. When I called to follow up, she was honest: "The other dealership responded in fifteen minutes. You took over an hour. I figured they wanted my business more."

That experience taught me that speed signals respect. When customers reach out digitally, they're often contacting multiple dealerships simultaneously. Your response time communicates whether you value their interest. But speed alone isn't enough—your response must also demonstrate that you actually read their inquiry and care about their specific situation.

Crafting Responses That Build Trust Digitally

The worst digital responses are the ones customers can immediately identify as templates: "Thank you for your interest in our dealership. We have a wide selection of vehicles. Please call us at your earliest convenience." These generic replies tell customers you didn't bother reading what they wrote and you're not interested in addressing their actual questions.

Effective digital responses follow a simple framework: acknowledge specifically what they asked about, answer their questions directly, add value they didn't request, and propose a clear next step. When a customer asks about a specific vehicle's fuel economy, don't just recite the EPA numbers they've already seen online. Explain what that means in real-world driving based on your experience with customers who own that model. When they inquire about pricing, provide transparent information while explaining what's included—warranty coverage, maintenance packages, or services that add value beyond the sticker price.

The channel matters significantly. Email allows for detailed responses with links to additional resources, virtual tours, or comparison information. Text messages should be conversational and concise—think of texting a friend rather than composing a formal letter. Live chat requires immediate engagement and a willingness to have a real-time conversation, not just push scripted responses.

Converting Digital Interest Into Showroom Visits

The ultimate goal of every digital response is moving the customer toward an in-person experience, but this requires finesse. Customers who've invested time researching online appreciate when you respect that effort rather than dismissing it.[14][15] I've found success by acknowledging their research: "It sounds like you've done thorough homework on this model. The questions you're asking tell me you understand what matters. I'd love to show you how the features you've researched actually work in person—there are a few things that are hard to appreciate until you experience them yourself."

Propose specific options rather than vague invitations. Instead of "Come by anytime," offer "I have availability tomorrow at 2 PM or Thursday at 10 AM—which works better for you?" This makes it easier for customers to commit because you've removed the friction of coordinating schedules.

When customers don't respond to your initial reply, follow up once within twenty-four hours with additional value—perhaps a video walk-around of the specific vehicle they inquired about, or information about a feature you forgot to mention. If they still don't respond, respect their silence. Persistent follow-ups feel desperate and damage the trust you're trying to build.

The sales professionals who excel at digital inquiry response understand they're not just answering questions—they're beginning relationships with people who've chosen to reach out.[16] Every email, text, and chat message is an opportunity to demonstrate the consultative, respectful approach that differentiates you from competitors still treating digital leads as interruptions rather than opportunities.[14][15][17]

Adding Value Beyond Information: What Customers Still Need From Sales Professionals in the Digital Age

Florence's initial reaction was defensive. For years, her expertise had been rooted in knowing more than the customer—about inventory, about features, about pricing structures. Now this stranger was telling her he'd done her job before even meeting her. Her instinct, honed over a decade and a half, was to challenge his information or redirect the conversation to areas where she still held advantage. But something stopped her.

Instead, she surprised both of them by saying, "That's impressive research. What sources did you use?" The young man, whose name was Marcus, seemed taken aback by her genuine interest. He explained his process: he'd spent two weeks reading reviews on multiple automotive websites, comparing specifications, watching video reviews, checking dealer invoice prices on consumer sites, and soliciting quotes via email from six dealerships within a fifty-mile radius.[58][59][60]

"So you've done your homework," Florence acknowledged. "I'm curious— if you have all that information, what brought you here in person?" It was a sincere question, not a sales tactic. She genuinely wanted to understand what role she could possibly play for a customer who seemed to need nothing from her.

Marcus hesitated, then admitted something that would reshape Florence's entire approach to modern sales: "Honestly? I'm overwhelmed. I have so much information that I'm not sure I'm making the right decision. I know the facts, but I don't know what they mean for me specifically. And I'm about to spend thirty thousand dollars, which is terrifying."

That moment crystallized a truth Florence had been sensing but hadn't articulated: the digital age hadn't eliminated the need for sales professionals—it had transformed what customers needed from them.[57][58][60] Marcus didn't need her to tell him the vehicle's horsepower or fuel economy; that information was readily available. What he needed was someone to help him translate data into confidence, to validate his research, to answer questions that couldn't be addressed by specification sheets, and to provide the human reassurance that comes from working with someone who has guided hundreds of people through this same decision.[57][60]

This represents the fundamental shift in automotive sales value proposition. While customers arrive armed with information that once existed exclusively in salespeople's minds, they simultaneously arrive drowning in data without context.[58][59][60] They've read conflicting reviews and don't know which to trust. They understand specifications but question whether those numbers translate to the right choice for their specific commute, family size, or lifestyle. They've calculated payments but worry about hidden costs or whether they're making a sound financial decision.

Your irreplaceable value in the digital age comes from providing what algorithms cannot: experiential wisdom from working with hundreds of similar buyers, real-world context for how features actually perform beyond marketing claims, validation that their research conclusions are sound, and the emotional reassurance that their significant investment makes sense.[57][60] You're no longer the information gatekeeper—you're the translator who helps customers convert their research into confident decisions.[57][60]

This also means addressing concerns that websites can't anticipate.[60] When Marcus mentioned he'd read mixed reviews about a particular feature,

Florence offered to demonstrate it during a test drive so he could evaluate it himself rather than relying on others' opinions.[58][60] When he showed her competing quotes on his phone, she didn't dismiss them or immediately try to beat them; instead, she asked what factors beyond price mattered to him in choosing a dealership—opening a conversation about relationship, service quality, and long-term support that no pricing website could address.[57][60][61]

The sales professionals who thrive with digitally-informed customers recognize that their role has elevated, not diminished. You're no longer competing with the internet as an information source—you're partnering with informed customers to help them navigate complexity, validate conclusions, experience what research alone cannot provide, and gain confidence that their decision is sound.[57][58][60] That human element remains irreplaceable, regardless of how sophisticated digital tools become.[57][60][61]

Leveraging Technology on the Showroom Floor: Using Digital Tools to Enhance Rather Than Replace Human Connection

Florence shifted her entire approach. Instead of trying to impress Marcus with information he already had, she asked about his specific situation: his commute, his lifestyle, his concerns, his previous vehicle experiences. When he mentioned he'd read mixed reviews about a particular feature, she offered to demonstrate it during a test drive so he could evaluate it himself rather than relying on others' opinions. When he showed her the competing quotes on his phone, she didn't dismiss them or immediately try to beat them; instead, she asked what factors beyond price mattered to him in choosing a dealership.

"I want to buy from someone I trust," Marcus said. "Someone who'll be here if something goes wrong. Someone who isn't just trying to beat me in a negotiation." Florence realized that while Marcus had successfully eliminated information asymmetry through his research, he couldn't eliminate uncertainty about the human element of the transaction.

Over the next two hours, Florence demonstrated a completely different skill set than she'd relied on for most of her career. She validated Marcus's research when it was accurate, gently corrected misconceptions when they arose, and most importantly, she helped him test his assumptions against real-world experience. During the test drive, she remained mostly quiet, letting him focus on how the vehicle felt rather than filling the silence with sales talk. When they returned, she pulled up the exact configuration he wanted on her computer, turned the screen toward him, and walked through every cost component with complete transparency.

This moment illustrates the essence of leveraging technology effectively on the showroom floor: using digital tools as collaborative instruments that enhance trust rather than barriers that separate you from customers. The tablet, computer, or smartphone in your hand isn't there to prove you're right—it's there to explore possibilities together, validate customer research, and create transparency that builds confidence.

I've watched dealerships invest heavily in digital signage, interactive kiosks, and sophisticated inventory systems, then wonder why these tools don't translate to increased sales.[65][66] The answer is simple: technology deployed to impress rarely works as well as technology deployed to collaborate. When Florence turned her screen toward Marcus, she transformed a potential power dynamic—where she controlled information—into a partnership where they examined data together.

The most effective showroom technology applications I've seen follow this collaborative principle. Sales professionals use tablets during test drives to pull up real-time comparisons when customers ask how a vehicle stacks up against competitors—not to dismiss the competition, but to provide objective data that helps customers make informed decisions. They use configurator tools on large displays to build vehicles alongside customers, visualizing options in real-time rather than describing them abstractly.[65][66] They leverage CRM systems to recall previous conversations and preferences, demonstrating that they've listened and remembered rather than treating each interaction as starting from zero.[62][68]

Digital tools also excel at addressing the transparency customers crave. When discussing pricing, pulling up invoice data, current incentives, and market comparisons on a screen you both can see eliminates the suspicion that you're hiding information. When explaining financing options, using digital calculators that show how different terms, down payments, and interest rates affect total cost empowers customers to make choices that genuinely fit their budget rather than accepting whatever you propose.[64]

The key distinction is this: technology should make you more human, not less. It should free you from memorizing every specification so you can focus on understanding what matters to each specific customer. It should provide visual confirmation of what you're explaining, building trust through transparency. It should enable you to respond immediately to questions—pulling up reviews, demonstrating features through videos, or connecting to inventory systems—without leaving customers waiting while you "check with someone."

But technology becomes counterproductive when it replaces conversation. I've seen salespeople so focused on their tablets that they miss the customer's body language signaling confusion or concern. I've watched presentations where the salesperson narrates a slick digital presentation while the customer sits passively, creating a one-way information dump rather than a collaborative exploration. The screen should facilitate dialogue, not substitute for it.[63][67]

Marcus ultimately purchased from Florence not because she had better technology than competing dealerships, but because she used technology to enhance their human connection—turning her computer into a shared resource, her smartphone into a tool for answering his questions in real-time, and digital pricing tools into instruments of transparency rather than negotiation leverage. The technology didn't replace Florence's expertise, empathy, or relationship-building—it amplified them, making her more effective at providing what Marcus actually needed: confidence in his decision backed by both data and human guidance.[62]

Bridging Online Research and In-Person Experience: Techniques for Validating Customer Research While Guiding the Decision

"Your research on our cost is pretty close," Florence told Marcus. "Here's our actual invoice, here's the holdback, here's what we need to make on the deal to keep the lights on. I'm not going to play games with you because you've clearly done the work to know when someone's being straight with you."

This moment—where Florence validated Marcus's research rather than dismissing or competing with it—represents the bridge between online preparation and in-person decision-making. The customers who arrive with smartphones full of data aren't looking for you to prove them wrong. They're looking for confirmation that their conclusions are sound, clarification where confusion exists, and confidence that the significant investment they're about to make is the right choice.

The validation process begins with a simple but powerful question: "What have you already discovered in your research?" This invitation accomplishes multiple objectives simultaneously. It demonstrates respect for the effort customers have invested, reveals what information they're working with, uncovers any misconceptions that need gentle correction, and establishes you as a collaborative partner rather than an adversary with competing information.[16]

When customers share their findings, resist the instinct to immediately correct or challenge them. I learned this the hard way early in my career when a customer mentioned reading that a particular model had "poor reliability ratings." My immediate response—"That's not accurate at all"—put him on the defensive and damaged the trust I was trying to build. What I should have said was: "I'm curious where you saw that, because the data I'm familiar with shows something different. Let me pull up the actual reliability reports so we can look at them together."

The distinction matters enormously. The first response positions you against the customer's research. The second positions you alongside them, examining information collaboratively. When you pull up third-party reliability data, owner satisfaction surveys, or safety ratings on a screen you both can see, you're not lecturing—you're exploring together.

Validation doesn't mean agreeing with everything customers present. It means taking their research seriously enough to engage with it honestly. When Marcus showed Florence competing quotes, she didn't immediately promise to beat them. She acknowledged they were legitimate, explained why pricing differences existed, and helped him understand what he'd receive for the price differential—warranty coverage, service quality, ongoing support—that quote sheets couldn't capture.

This approach transforms the in-person experience from information delivery to decision facilitation. Your role isn't repeating specifications customers have already memorized; it's providing context those specifications don't convey. When a customer mentions a vehicle's fuel economy rating, you can share what actual owners report in real-world driving conditions. When they ask about a safety feature they've read about, you can demonstrate how it functions in practice during the test drive. When they've calculated payments online, you can explore how different term lengths, down payments, or timing affect their total cost in ways generic calculators cannot personalize.

The test drive becomes particularly valuable for validating research. Encourage customers to specifically evaluate the features or concerns they've read about online. If they've seen mixed reviews about visibility, have them navigate the parking lot and assess sight lines themselves. If they've read about advanced driver assistance systems, demonstrate them in real traffic conditions. The physical experience either confirms their research or reveals nuances that online reviews couldn't capture for their specific needs and preferences.

Throughout this process, your expertise manifests not in knowing more than the customer, but in having guided hundreds of similar buyers through this same decision.[17] You've seen which online concerns translate to real-world issues and which fade once customers experience the vehicle firsthand. You understand how different customers with different priorities have evaluated the same information and reached different conclusions. That experiential wisdom—accumulated across countless transactions—is what customers cannot replicate through research alone, and it's what makes your role irreplaceable in the digital age.## Conclusion: Your Evolving Role in the Digital Marketplace

The transformation Florence experienced—from defensive information-gatekeeper to collaborative guide—mirrors the evolution every automotive sales professional must embrace to remain relevant in today's marketplace. The digitally-informed customer hasn't made your role obsolete; they've clarified what genuine value looks like when information is no longer scarce.

Marcus arrived at Florence's dealership with extensive research, competitive quotes, and detailed knowledge, yet he still needed something fundamental that no website could provide: human guidance through complexity, validation that his conclusions were sound, and confidence that his significant investment made sense for his specific situation. This pattern repeats across every showroom in America—customers drowning in data but thirsting for wisdom, armed with facts but seeking reassurance, informed about vehicles but uncertain about decisions.

Your competitive advantage in this environment comes not from knowing more than customers, but from having guided hundreds of similar buyers through this same journey. You've seen which online concerns translate to real-world issues and which fade during test drives. You understand how different priorities lead different customers to different conclusions from identical research. You can provide the experiential context, real-world validation, and personalized guidance that algorithms cannot replicate, no matter how sophisticated they become.

The techniques explored in this chapter—responding promptly and personally to digital inquiries, adding value beyond information through consultative conversation, leveraging technology as a collaborative tool rather than a barrier, and validating customer research while guiding decisions—represent more than tactical adjustments. They reflect a fundamental mindset shift from competing with the internet to partnering with informed customers, from controlling information flow to facilitating confident decision-making, from proving your expertise to demonstrating your commitment to their success.

This approach requires vulnerability that may feel uncomfortable initially. When you acknowledge that a competitor's quote is legitimate, when you validate research that contradicts your assumptions, when you turn your screen toward customers to examine data together, you're surrendering the information asymmetry that once defined automotive sales power dynamics. But that surrender isn't weakness—it's the foundation of the trust that digitally-informed customers desperately seek and rarely find.

The sales professionals who thrive in this environment understand that every digital inquiry, every research-armed customer, every smartphone consultation during your conversation represents opportunity rather than threat. These customers have already invested significant time and energy into their purchase journey. They've demonstrated genuine interest by reaching out. Your job isn't convincing them they need a vehicle—it's helping them feel confident about which vehicle, which dealership, and which salesperson deserve their business and their trust.

As you implement these strategies, remember Florence's pivotal realization: the digital age didn't eliminate the need for automotive sales professionals—it elevated what customers need from them. The question isn't whether you're still relevant, but whether you've adapted to provide what modern buyers actually require. Master that adaptation, and you'll discover that digitally-informed customers aren't your most challenging prospects—they're your most qualified ones, already substantially through their journey and needing only what you're uniquely positioned to provide: the human element that transforms research into confidence and information into decisions.

Chapter 5

Automotive Objection Handling: Transforming Resistance into Opportunity

O bjections are not rejections—they're invitations to understand what's standing between your customer and the confidence they need to move forward. The sales professional who learns to welcome resistance rather than fear it discovers that every objection contains valuable information about unmet needs, unresolved concerns, or unexplored solutions. Objections are not rejections—they're invitations to understand what's standing between your customer and the confidence they need to move forward. The sales professional who learns to welcome resistance rather than fear it discovers that every objection contains valuable information about unmet needs, unresolved concerns, or unexplored solutions.

For most of my career, I watched salespeople treat objections like enemies to defeat—obstacles standing between them and their commission. The moment a customer said "I need to think about it" or "That's more than I wanted to spend," these salespeople would launch into rehearsed rebuttals designed to overcome resistance through clever wordplay or psychological pressure. They'd been trained to view objections as problems requiring immediate solutions, battles demanding tactical victories. What they failed to recognize was that this adversarial approach often pushed away the very customers who were closest to buying.

The transformation in how I understood objection handling came from a simple realization: customers who raise objections are still engaged in the conversation. They haven't walked away. They're telling you exactly what's preventing them from moving forward, offering you a roadmap to help them reach a decision they'll feel genuinely good about. When someone says "I'm worried about the monthly payment," they're not rejecting your vehicle—they're sharing a legitimate financial concern that deserves exploration rather than dismissal. When they say "I want to compare this with what the dealership across town is offering," they're not playing games—they're doing responsible research that you should respect and work with rather than against.

This chapter will equip you with practical frameworks for transforming objections from roadblocks into opportunities for deeper understanding and genuine problem-solving. You'll learn to distinguish between surface-level objections—the polite concerns customers voice first—and the underlying hesitations that actually drive their resistance. We'll explore the five most common objections you'll encounter on the showroom floor: concerns about price, monthly payment, timing, trade-in value, and decision-making authority. More importantly, you'll discover what these objections actually mean and how to address them through collaborative conversation rather than combative tactics.

The Listen-Acknowledge-Explore framework you'll master in this chapter replaces the outdated "overcome and close" mentality with a consultative approach that honors customer intelligence while guiding them toward confidence. You'll learn specific language patterns and questioning techniques that uncover the real concerns hiding beneath initial objections, allowing you to address what's actually holding customers back rather than what they first mention. By the end of this chapter, you'll understand how to turn "I need to think about it"—the objection that sends most salespeople into panic mode—into a productive conversation that either resolves hidden concerns or respectfully acknowledges when a customer genuinely needs time to process a significant decision.

The goal isn't to eliminate objections or manipulate customers past their hesitations. The goal is to become the kind of sales professional customers trust enough to share their real concerns with, knowing you'll help them work through legitimate obstacles rather than pressure them past their better judgment.

Understanding the Psychology Behind Objections: Why Customers Resist and What They're Really Telling You

I learned something crucial about objections during my third year on the showroom floor that completely changed how I approached resistance. A customer named Robert spent forty-five minutes with me, test-drove a truck he clearly loved, and then said the words that used to make my stomach drop: "I need to think about it." My instinct—honed by traditional training—was to launch into objection-handling scripts designed to "overcome" his resistance. Instead, I simply asked, "What specifically do you need to think through?"

Robert paused, surprised by the question. Then he admitted something that revealed the gap between what customers say and what they actually mean: "Honestly? My wife and I agreed we'd make this decision together, and I feel guilty that I'm this excited about a truck without her input." His objection had nothing to do with the vehicle, the price, or our dealership. It was about relationship dynamics and shared decision-making— something no scripted rebuttal could address.

That moment taught me that objections are rarely about what customers initially say they're about. They're coded messages revealing deeper concerns, fears, or unmet needs that customers themselves may not fully recognize or feel comfortable articulating directly.[69][70][71]

The Fear Behind the Words

When customers resist, they're almost always experiencing some form of fear—even if they'd never describe it that way. Fear of making a costly mistake. Fear of buyer's remorse. Fear of being taken advantage of. Fear of judgment from family or friends. Fear of commitment to a multi-year financial obligation.[69][70] These fears manifest as seemingly rational objections about price, timing, features, or the need to "shop around," but addressing only the surface concern leaves the underlying fear untouched.

Research in consumer psychology consistently demonstrates that major purchases trigger what psychologists call "cognitive dissonance"—the mental discomfort that arises when making decisions involving risk or uncertainty. For most customers, a vehicle purchase represents the second-largest financial commitment they'll make after buying a home. That level of investment naturally activates protective psychological mechanisms designed to prevent mistakes.[69][70]

Understanding this helps explain why customers who seem completely satisfied with a vehicle suddenly raise objections at the closing stage. It's not that they've discovered new problems—it's that the psychological weight of commitment has triggered their internal warning systems.[72] Their brain is essentially saying, "This is a big decision. Are you absolutely certain?"

The Trust Deficit

Every customer who walks onto your lot carries invisible baggage from previous experiences—their own negative car-buying stories, horror tales from friends and family, and cultural narratives about "sleazy car salespeople" that have persisted for decades.[69] This creates what I call the trust deficit: customers start from a position of skepticism rather than neutral evaluation.

When someone says "I want to shop around" or "I can probably get a better deal elsewhere," they're often not making a factual statement about pricing. They're expressing their uncertainty about whether they can trust you, your dealership, and the deal you're presenting.[69][70] The objection is a defense mechanism—a way of maintaining control and protecting themselves from potential manipulation.[69][71]

This is why transparency and authenticity matter so profoundly in modern automotive sales. Customers aren't just evaluating vehicles and prices; they're constantly assessing whether you're trustworthy.[69][71] Every interaction either builds or erodes that trust, and objections often arise at the precise moment when trust hasn't been sufficiently established to support the level of commitment you're requesting.

What They're Really Asking

Behind virtually every objection lies an unspoken question customers need answered before they can move forward with confidence.[69][70][71] "The price is too high" often means "I'm not convinced the value justifies this investment—help me understand what I'm getting."[69][72] "I need to talk to my spouse" frequently translates to "I need emotional support for this decision" or "I'm afraid of making this choice alone."[69][71] "It's not the right time" usually signals "I'm uncertain about my financial situation" or "I need a compelling reason to act now rather than later."[72]

The sales professional who learns to hear these underlying questions— rather than just the surface objections—gains a profound advantage.[69][71] You stop defending and start exploring. You stop convincing and start understanding. Most importantly, you stop treating objections as obstacles to overcome and start recognizing them as invitations to address what's genuinely holding your customer back from a decision they'll feel great about.[69][71]

The Five Most Common Automotive Objections and What They Actually Mean: Price, Payment, Timing, Trade Value, and Decision Authority

Walk into any dealership training room, and you'll find salespeople memorizing rebuttals to objections—scripted responses designed to counter customer resistance with clever wordplay. But here's what I learned after handling thousands of objections: the specific words customers use matter far less than understanding what they're actually trying to communicate.[73][69] Five objections account for roughly 90% of the resistance you'll encounter, and each one tells a story that goes much deeper than the surface concern.

Price: "That's More Than I Want to Spend"

When customers object to price, they're rarely making a mathematical statement. They're expressing uncertainty about value, revealing budget anxiety, or testing whether you've given them your best offer.[69] I once had a customer tell me a vehicle was "too expensive" while wearing a watch that cost more than the down payment. His objection wasn't about affordability—it was about whether he believed the vehicle was worth the investment relative to alternatives.

The digitally-informed customer has likely seen pricing from multiple sources before arriving at your dealership.[73] When they say "that's too high," they often mean "I saw it listed for less online" or "I'm not convinced this is fair based on my research."[73] [69] Your response shouldn't be immediate discounting—it should be collaborative exploration. Ask what price they were expecting and what that's based on. Show them how you arrived at your number. Help them understand the difference between advertised prices that exclude fees and the actual transaction price they'll pay anywhere.

Sometimes price objections mask payment concerns. A customer focused on monthly budget may express sticker shock at the total price when their real question is "can I afford the payments?" This is why clarifying questions matter more than rehearsed rebuttals.

Payment: "The Monthly Payment Is Too High"

Payment objections reveal budget realities and financing anxiety.[69] Unlike price objections, which are often negotiating tactics, payment concerns usually reflect genuine financial constraints. When someone says "I can't afford $500 a month," believe them. Your job isn't to convince them they can—it's to explore whether there's a structure that actually works for their situation.[69]

This might mean longer terms, larger down payments, or frankly, a less expensive vehicle.[69] I've built some of my strongest customer relationships by helping people find vehicles that fit their budget rather than stretching them into payments that would create stress. One customer I guided toward a certified pre-owned vehicle instead of the new model she'd initially wanted sent me four referrals over the next year because I'd prioritized her financial comfort over my commission.

Timing: "I'm Not Ready to Buy Today"

Timing objections are the most misunderstood. Traditional sales training treats "I need to think about it" as a smokescreen requiring aggressive closing tactics. But in my experience, timing resistance usually signals one of three things: unresolved concerns about the vehicle or deal, lack of urgency, or genuine need for processing time on a major decision.[69]

Your response should determine which category you're dealing with. Ask directly: "What specifically do you need to think through?" If they cite concrete concerns—insurance costs, comparing features, checking with a mechanic—those are legitimate needs you can help address.[69] If they're vague or evasive, you may be dealing with unspoken objections about price, value, or trust that require more exploration.[69]

Creating urgency without manipulation means highlighting genuine scarcity or time-sensitive opportunities.[69] If a vehicle is genuinely in high demand or an incentive truly expires soon, share that information transparently. But manufactured urgency destroys trust.

Trade Value: "My Trade Is Worth More"

Trade-in objections almost always stem from the gap between online valuations and real-world offers.[69] Customers see Kelley Blue Book's "excellent condition" number and believe that's what they should receive, not understanding how condition assessments, market demand, and reconditioning costs affect actual value.

Walk customers through your evaluation process.[69] Show them the comparable sales data you're using. Explain specifically what condition factors affected the appraisal. Transparency doesn't always close the gap, but it builds understanding and trust that facilitate agreement.

Decision Authority: "I Need to Talk to My Spouse"

When customers cite absent decision-makers, they're either genuinely sharing authority with someone not present or using this as a polite exit strategy.[69] The difference is usually obvious from context and body language. If they've been engaged and enthusiastic throughout the process, they probably do need spousal input. If they've seemed hesitant or uncommitted, the absent spouse is likely a convenient objection masking deeper concerns.[69]

For genuine shared decision-making, offer to include the other party via phone or video call, or schedule a time when both can return.[69] For polite exits disguised as spousal consultation, circle back to exploring what's really holding them back: "I completely understand wanting to discuss this together. Before you go, is there anything about the vehicle or the deal that concerns you? I want to make sure we've addressed everything so your conversation at home is productive."

Understanding what objections actually mean transforms how you respond—from combative rebuttal to collaborative problem-solving.[73][69]

The Listen-Acknowledge-Explore Framework: A Consultative Alternative to Traditional Objection 'Handling'

I discovered the power of this framework during my seventh year in automotive sales, when a customer named Patricia taught me that the word "handling" itself was part of the problem. She'd been working with me for about thirty minutes when I attempted what I'd been trained to do—counter her price objection with a rehearsed value statement. She stopped me mid-sentence and said, "I don't need you to handle me. I need you to help me figure this out." That moment crystallized something I'd been sensing but couldn't articulate: objections aren't problems requiring handling—they're conversations requiring partnership.

The Listen-Acknowledge-Explore-Respond framework transforms objections from adversarial moments into collaborative problem-solving opportunities.[79] Unlike traditional objection "handling" techniques that position you against the customer, LAER positions you alongside them, working together to address legitimate concerns that stand between them and a confident decision.

Listen: Beyond Hearing to Understanding

Genuine listening means resisting every instinct to formulate your response while the customer is speaking.[75 77 78] When someone says "I'm concerned about the monthly payment," most salespeople immediately begin calculating different term lengths or down payment scenarios. But authentic listening requires you to remain present, maintain eye contact, and—most importantly—stay silent after they finish speaking.[75 78]

I learned to count to five in my head after a customer completes their objection. That silence accomplishes two critical things: it gives them space to elaborate on what they really mean, and it demonstrates that you're genuinely processing their concern rather than waiting for your turn to talk.[78] Patricia, the customer who changed my perspective, added crucial context during that silence: "My daughter starts college next year, and I'm worried about overextending." Without that silence, I would have missed the real concern entirely.

Acknowledge: Validation Without Agreement

Acknowledgment is not concession.[78] When you say "I understand that monthly payment is a significant consideration for you," you're validating that their concern is legitimate and worthy of attention—you're not agreeing that the payment is too high or that you need to lower it.

The language of acknowledgment matters enormously.[78] Phrases like "I appreciate you sharing that" or "That's an important consideration" communicate respect without defensiveness.[76] What you're really saying is: "Your concern is real, and I'm taking it seriously." This simple act of validation often defuses the tension that makes objections feel adversarial.[76]

Explore: Uncovering the Real Story

Exploration transforms the conversation from debate to discovery.[75][77] Instead of countering Patricia's payment concern with financing options, I asked: "Help me understand what you're comfortable with monthly, and what's driving that number for you?" Her answer revealed that she'd calculated her budget based on maintaining her current savings rate for college expenses—information that completely reframed how I could help her.

Effective exploration questions include: "What specifically concerns you about that?" or "Can you tell me more about what you're thinking?" or "What would need to be different for this to work for you?"[77] These open-ended questions invite customers to share the context, constraints, and priorities that inform their objections.

The goal isn't to interrogate—it's to understand the complete picture so your response addresses their actual situation rather than your assumption about their objection.[74][75]

Respond: Tailored Solutions, Not Generic Rebuttals

Only after listening completely, acknowledging genuinely, and exploring thoroughly should you craft a response.[75][77] This response is now informed by real understanding rather than guesswork.

For Patricia, my response became: "Based on what you've shared about college expenses, what if we structured this differently? We could look at a certified pre-owned vehicle that meets your needs at a lower payment, preserving your savings plan. Or we could explore a shorter term with slightly higher payments now, so you own the vehicle outright before college costs peak." Neither option was a generic rebuttal—both were tailored solutions addressing her specific situation.[77]

The LAER framework doesn't eliminate objections, but it transforms them from obstacles into opportunities to demonstrate that you're genuinely invested in finding solutions that work for your customer's real life, not just closing a deal.

Addressing Price Objections Without Devaluing Your Product or Destroying Trust

Price objections are inevitable, but how you respond determines whether you build trust or destroy it. I learned this lesson the hard way during my fourth year in automotive sales when a customer named Marcus walked in, test-drove a vehicle he clearly loved, and then said flatly, "I can get this same car for two thousand dollars less at the dealership across town." My instinct—trained by old-school managers—was to immediately discount or attack the competitor's credibility. Instead, I took a breath and said something that felt risky: "Let's look at that offer together."

Marcus pulled up the competitor's online listing on his phone, and we examined it side by side with our vehicle.[82] Within two minutes, the differences became clear: their vehicle had 8,000 more miles, lacked the premium sound system Marcus wanted, and didn't include our lifetime powertrain warranty.[82] Marcus hadn't been lying or playing games—he'd genuinely found a lower price and needed help understanding why ours was higher. By treating his objection as legitimate rather than adversarial, I preserved both the vehicle's value and his trust.[82] He bought that day and has since referred three customers to me.

The Transparency Principle

When customers challenge your price, your first instinct might be to defend, discount, or deflect. Resist all three.[82][69] Instead, embrace radical transparency about how you arrived at your number. Show them the invoice if they ask. Walk them through the equipment differences between your vehicle and the competitor's.[82] Explain market factors affecting pricing—supply constraints, demand for specific colors or configurations, regional variations.

This transparency doesn't weaken your position; it strengthens it.[80] Customers who understand your pricing logic stop viewing you as an adversary trying to extract maximum profit and start seeing you as a partner helping them make an informed decision. One technique I use consistently: turn my computer screen toward the customer and pull up the same pricing tools they've likely already consulted online. When they see you're using the same data sources they trust, skepticism transforms into collaboration.

Reframe Value, Don't Reduce Price

The fastest way to devalue your product is to drop your price without justification.[82][69] Every time you discount reflexively, you teach customers that your initial price was inflated and that persistence pays off. This creates a negotiation dynamic where trust evaporates and every transaction becomes a battle.

Instead, reframe the conversation from price to value.[69] When someone says "that's too expensive," they're really saying "I don't see enough value to justify this investment."[80] Your job isn't to lower the price—it's to illuminate value they haven't recognized. Ask questions that reveal what matters most to them: safety features for their family, reliability for their commute, technology that simplifies their life, fuel efficiency that saves money over time.[81 82 69]

I once worked with a customer named Jennifer who balked at the price of a hybrid SUV. Rather than discounting, I asked about her daily driving patterns. She commuted sixty miles round-trip. I pulled up a fuel cost calculator and showed her that over five years of ownership, she'd save nearly $8,000 in fuel costs compared to the non-hybrid alternative she was considering. The monthly payment was $75 higher, but her monthly fuel savings would be $110. Suddenly the "expensive" vehicle became the economical choice.[80 69] She didn't need a lower price—she needed a clearer understanding of total cost of ownership.[82 69]

When to Walk Away

Sometimes the most trust-building response to a price objection is acknowledging when you genuinely can't meet a customer's budget.[80 81] I've told customers, "Based on what you've shared about your budget, I don't think this vehicle is the right fit right now. Let me show you something that works better for where you are financially." This honesty has generated more referrals than any closing technique I've ever used.

Customers remember salespeople who prioritized their financial wellbeing over a commission. That memory becomes the foundation of long-term relationships worth far more than any single sale.

Turning 'I Need to Think About It' Into Productive Conversation: Uncovering and Resolving Hidden Concerns

"I need to think about it" used to send a jolt of panic through my chest during my early years in automotive sales. I'd been trained to view those six words as a polite rejection—a customer's way of saying "no" without confrontation. My managers would huddle with me immediately, strategizing ways to "overcome" this objection with urgency tactics or last-minute concessions. But I learned something crucial after hundreds of these interactions: customers who say they need to think about it are actually giving you a gift.[81][69] They're still engaged in the conversation, still considering the purchase, and—most importantly—they're telling you exactly what they need from you, even if they don't realize it themselves.

The transformation in how I approached this objection came from a customer named David who'd spent three hours with me over two visits. He loved the vehicle, the numbers worked for his budget, and he'd even brought his wife for her approval on the second visit. When I asked if he was ready to move forward, he said those familiar words: "I just need to think about it." Instead of launching into closing tactics, I asked a simple question that changed everything: "That makes complete sense. Can I ask—what specifically do you want to think through?"[81]

David paused, clearly not expecting the question. Then he admitted something profound: "Honestly, I'm not sure. Everything seems right, but I feel like I'm missing something." That vulnerability opened a conversation that revealed his real concern—he'd never financed a vehicle before and felt anxious about committing to a five-year loan, even though the payment fit comfortably in his budget. His objection wasn't about the vehicle, the price, or our dealership. It was about fear of long-term financial commitment that he hadn't articulated because he felt it might sound foolish.[80][69]

The Hidden Concerns Behind the Hesitation

When customers say they need to think about it, they're rarely stalling for time to comparison shop, despite what traditional sales training suggests. Research in consumer psychology demonstrates that major purchase decisions trigger what's called "approach-avoidance conflict"—the simultaneous desire to move forward and fear of making a mistake. For automotive purchases, this conflict intensifies because customers are committing to years of payments for a depreciating asset while navigating an industry they've been culturally conditioned to distrust.

The hidden concerns typically fall into several categories. **Financial anxiety** extends beyond whether they can afford the payment to whether they should—worries about job security, competing financial priorities, or past experiences with buyer's remorse.[83][81] **Decision-making authority** issues arise when customers need spousal approval, want to consult family members, or feel pressure from others who aren't present. **Value uncertainty** manifests when customers aren't fully convinced the vehicle justifies the investment, even if they can't articulate specific shortcomings.[80][69] **Commitment fear** surfaces around the permanence of the decision and the difficulty of reversing it if circumstances change.[80][69]

Understanding these categories transforms how you respond. Instead of treating "I need to think about it" as resistance to overcome, you recognize it as an invitation to explore what's actually holding them back.[81][69]

The Exploration Framework

The most effective response begins with genuine curiosity rather than scripted rebuttals. When David admitted he wasn't sure what he needed to think through, I could have dismissed his concern or pressured him to decide. Instead, I explored collaboratively: "Sometimes when we feel uncertain but can't pinpoint why, it's because there's a question we haven't fully answered yet. What questions are still on your mind about this vehicle or this decision?"[83][81]

This open-ended exploration accomplishes several things simultaneously. It demonstrates respect for their decision-making process, positioning you as an advisor rather than an adversary.[80][81] It gives customers permission to voice concerns they might have felt were trivial or embarrassing.[84] Most importantly, it surfaces the real obstacles so you can address them directly rather than guessing.[83][81]

For David, my follow-up questions revealed that he'd never calculated the total interest he'd pay over the loan term and felt anxious about "hidden costs" he couldn't see. We spent fifteen minutes with a calculator, walking through the complete financial picture—total payments, interest costs, maintenance expenses, fuel savings compared to his current vehicle, and insurance differences. The transparency didn't eliminate his commitment anxiety, but it transformed vague fear into concrete information he could evaluate rationally.[80][81]

Addressing What You Uncover

Once you've identified the real concern, your response must be tailored and substantive, not generic reassurance. If financial anxiety emerges, explore whether restructuring the deal addresses it—different term lengths, larger down payments, or frankly, a less expensive vehicle that eliminates stress.[83] If decision-making authority is the issue, offer to include the absent party via phone call, provide materials they can review together, or schedule a time when everyone can be present.

When value uncertainty surfaces, return to needs assessment. What specific doubts do they have? Are there features they don't understand? Comparisons they want to explore? Sometimes customers need permission to test-drive again or spend more time with the vehicle to build confidence. I've had customers who needed to sit in the vehicle alone for ten minutes, imagining their daily commute, before they felt ready to commit.

The key is matching your response to their actual concern rather than deploying generic closing tactics.[80][83] David didn't need a discount or artificial urgency—he needed financial education and reassurance that he was making a sound decision. By addressing his real concern, I transformed his hesitation into confidence.[80][81] He purchased that day, but more importantly, he referred two friends over the next year, telling them I was "the first car salesperson who didn't make him feel pressured."

When Thinking About It Is Legitimate

Sometimes customers genuinely need time to process a major decision, and the most trust-building response is respecting that need.[80][81] After exploring their concerns and addressing what you can, if they still want time, give it to them without guilt or pressure. Set a specific follow-up: "I completely understand wanting to sleep on this. Can I check in with you tomorrow afternoon to answer any questions that come up?"[84] This maintains connection while honoring their process.

The customers who leave feeling respected and understood return at much higher rates than those who leave feeling pressured.[80][84] More importantly, they return as advocates rather than skeptics, having experienced a sales process that prioritized their confidence over your commission.[81] [69]Objections have taught me more about successful automotive sales than any other aspect of the profession. Every time a customer expresses hesitation, raises a concern, or pushes back against what I'm presenting, they're offering me something invaluable—a window into what they actually need to move forward with confidence. The sales professionals who thrive in today's market aren't those who've memorized the cleverest rebuttals or mastered the most aggressive closing tactics. They're the ones who've learned to welcome objections as collaborative problem-solving opportunities rather than adversarial confrontations.

Throughout this chapter, we've explored how objections reveal the psychological landscape beneath customer decision-making—the fears about making costly mistakes, the trust deficits created by industry reputation, and the legitimate concerns that deserve respect rather than dismissal. You've learned that when someone says "the price is too high," they're often asking you to help them understand value. When they say "I need to think about it," they're frequently signaling unresolved concerns they haven't yet articulated. When they mention trade-in value, payment amounts, timing, or absent decision-makers, they're providing you with a roadmap to guide them toward confidence if you're willing to listen rather than simply counter.

The Listen-Acknowledge-Explore-Respond framework transforms these moments from obstacles into opportunities. By genuinely listening beyond the surface objection, acknowledging concerns without defensiveness, exploring the real story behind initial resistance, and responding with tailored solutions rather than generic scripts, you position yourself as a partner in your customer's decision-making process rather than an adversary they need to defend against. This consultative approach doesn't just close more sales—it builds the kind of trust that generates referrals, repeat business, and long-term relationships that sustain careers through market changes and economic fluctuations.

The specific techniques we've covered—addressing price objections through transparency rather than immediate discounting, reframing value instead of reducing profit, uncovering hidden concerns behind "I need to think about it," and distinguishing between legitimate processing time and polite exit strategies—all share a common foundation. They work because they honor customer intelligence, respect genuine concerns, and prioritize finding solutions that customers feel genuinely good about long after the initial excitement of a new vehicle fades.

As you move forward in your automotive sales career, remember that objections aren't rejections. They're invitations to understand what's standing between your customer and the confidence they need. The moment someone raises a concern, they're still engaged in the conversation with you. They haven't walked away. They're telling you exactly what they need, even if they don't fully realize it themselves. Your job isn't to overcome their resistance through clever tactics or psychological pressure—it's to explore their concerns collaboratively, address what's genuinely holding them back, and help them reach decisions they'll feel empowered by both today and months from now when they're recommending you to friends and family.

The sales professionals who master this approach discover something powerful: resistance transforms from the most stressful part of the sales process into the most valuable. Every objection becomes an opportunity to demonstrate that you're on your customer's side, working with them rather than against them. That's when objections stop being obstacles and become the foundation of trust, loyalty, and sustainable success in modern automotive sales.

Chapter 6

Dealership Negotiation Tactics: Creating Win-Win Outcomes That Build Loyalty

Negotiation in automotive sales has long been misunderstood as a zero-sum game where every dollar the customer saves represents a dollar the dealership loses, and vice versa. This adversarial mindset creates transactions that one party regrets and relationships that end the moment the customer drives away, but a fundamentally different approach—one focused on creating mutual value—transforms negotiation into the foundation of lasting loyalty. Negotiation in automotive sales has long been misunderstood as a zero-sum game where every dollar the customer saves represents a dollar the dealership loses, and vice versa. This adversarial mindset creates transactions that one party regrets and relationships that end the moment the customer drives away, but a fundamentally different approach—one focused on creating mutual value—transforms negotiation into the foundation of lasting loyalty.

Throughout my years on dealership floors, I've watched countless sales professionals approach negotiation as a battle to be won rather than a problem to be solved collaboratively. They'd employ tactics designed to extract maximum profit from each transaction—holding back information, creating artificial scarcity, using confusing payment structures to obscure actual costs, or wearing customers down through extended back-and-forth with managers. These approaches occasionally produced impressive gross profits on individual deals, but they consistently destroyed something far more valuable: the customer's trust and willingness to return or refer others.

The shift I witnessed—and eventually embraced—wasn't about becoming "soft" on profit or giving away margin unnecessarily. It was about recognizing that negotiation built on transparency, honesty, and genuine problem-solving creates customers who feel genuinely good about their deals long after the initial excitement fades. These customers become advocates who generate referrals, return for their next vehicle purchase, and leave positive online reviews that attract new prospects. The math is compelling: a customer who feels manipulated during negotiation might generate one sale and zero referrals, while a customer who experiences collaborative negotiation might generate three to five sales over their lifetime through repeat business and referrals.

This chapter will equip you with specific negotiation frameworks that honor both dealership profitability and customer satisfaction. You'll learn how to structure pricing discussions transparently without destroying your negotiating position, how to handle trade-in valuations in ways customers understand and accept, how to respond to competitive quotes without immediately discounting or becoming defensive, and how to create deal structures that customers won't regret weeks or months later. These aren't theoretical concepts—they're practical techniques I've used and taught that work in real dealership environments with real customers who arrive armed with online research, competitive quotes, and healthy skepticism.

The negotiation strategies you'll discover here reflect what today's digitally-informed customers actually respond to. They've already researched pricing online, they know when they're being misled, and they have infinite options if they sense manipulation. The sales professional who can negotiate with integrity, transparency, and genuine concern for mutual benefit doesn't just close more deals—they build reputations that become their greatest competitive advantage, making future negotiations easier because trust precedes the conversation rather than having to be built from scratch each time.

The Win-Win Negotiation Framework: Moving Beyond Adversarial Tactics to Collaborative Problem-Solving

I learned the power of win-win negotiation not from a training manual, but from watching a deal fall apart that should have been easy. A customer named Robert had test-driven a truck, loved everything about it, and the numbers worked for both sides. But my colleague at the time treated the negotiation like a poker game—withholding information, creating artificial urgency, playing the "let me talk to my manager" routine multiple times. Robert eventually bought the truck, but I'll never forget what he said as he signed: "I got what I wanted, but I feel like I just survived a battle." He never returned for service, never referred anyone, and left a lukewarm review online. We won the negotiation but lost everything that mattered afterward.

The win-win framework operates on a fundamentally different premise: negotiation isn't about one party extracting maximum value from the other—it's about collaborative problem-solving where both dealership profitability and customer satisfaction are legitimate goals that can coexist.[88] [89] [90] This approach recognizes what research from Harvard's Program on Negotiation has consistently demonstrated: agreements where both parties feel satisfied produce better long-term outcomes than those where one side "wins" at the other's expense.[88]

Understanding Interests, Not Just Positions

The foundation of win-win negotiation is distinguishing between positions and interests. A customer's position might be "I want this truck for $35,000." Their underlying interest might be "I need monthly payments under $500 because of my budget constraints" or "I want to feel confident I'm getting fair market value." When you focus on interests rather than positions, creative solutions emerge that satisfy both parties.[88] [90]

I once worked with a customer named Lisa who was adamant about a specific price point that was genuinely below our cost on a particular SUV. Instead of simply saying no or trying to wear her down, I asked, "Help me understand what's driving that number for you." She explained she'd calculated her maximum based on keeping her total car expenses— payment, insurance, and fuel—within a specific monthly budget. Once I understood her actual interest, we explored alternatives: a slightly different trim level that met her needs at a lower price point, extended financing terms that kept payments comfortable, and fuel-efficient options that reduced her operating costs.[85] [90] We structured a deal that worked for both of us because we focused on solving her real problem rather than battling over positions.

Transparency as a Negotiation Tool

Win-win negotiation requires transparency about constraints and possibilities.[85][86] When customers arrive with competitive quotes or online pricing research—which nearly all do today—acknowledge their information openly.[85][86] I've found that showing customers exactly how I'm calculating trade-in values, explaining market conditions affecting pricing, and being honest about what flexibility exists builds more trust than any negotiation tactic.[89]

One approach that consistently works: turn your computer screen toward the customer during pricing discussions. Show them the actual numbers you're working with—vehicle cost, market adjustments, available incentives. This transparency doesn't weaken your negotiating position; it strengthens the relationship by demonstrating you're working with them, not against them.[89]

Creating Value Beyond Price

Win-win outcomes often emerge when you expand the negotiation beyond purchase price alone.[85][86] Payment terms, trade-in timing, service packages, warranty options, and delivery scheduling all represent variables where you can create value.[85][90] A customer focused solely on lowest price might be equally satisfied with added services, extended warranties at cost, or flexible trade-in arrangements that solve other problems they're facing.[87][89][90]

The goal isn't manipulating customers into accepting less favorable terms disguised as "value." It's genuinely exploring what matters most to them and finding creative ways to address those priorities while maintaining dealership profitability.[87][89] When both parties leave feeling satisfied, you've created the foundation for referrals, repeat business, and the kind of positive online reviews that attract future customers who are predisposed to trust you before ever walking through your door.[88][89]

Transparent Pricing Strategies: Building Trust Through Honesty About Margins, Costs, and Value

I'll never forget the moment I realized that hiding pricing information was costing me more than it protected. A customer named Rachel had researched a crossover SUV for weeks, arrived with printouts of invoice pricing from multiple websites, and asked me directly: "What did you actually pay for this vehicle?" My instinct—trained by years of traditional sales culture—was to deflect, redirect to value, or give a vague answer. Instead, I made a choice that felt risky at the time: I pulled up our actual invoice on my computer, turned the screen toward her, and walked through every line item.

Rachel's shoulders visibly relaxed. "No one else would show me this," she said. "They all acted like I was asking for state secrets." That transparency didn't cost me profit—it eliminated three hours of negotiation dance, created immediate trust, and led to a sale at a fair margin for both of us.[91][94] More importantly, Rachel sent me four referrals over the next year, each one mentioning that I was "the only salesperson who was completely honest about pricing."[91][92][93][94]

The New Reality of Pricing Transparency

Today's car buyers arrive at dealerships armed with extensive pricing research. They've seen invoice costs on Edmunds and TrueCar, compared prices across dealer websites, and often have competitive quotes on their phones.[91][92][93] The Federal Trade Commission's increasing focus on clear fee disclosure and consumer protection means dealerships face both regulatory pressure and market demand for transparency.[91] Fighting this reality by withholding information doesn't protect your margins—it destroys trust before you've had a chance to build it.

Transparent pricing doesn't mean giving away profit or accepting whatever customers demand. It means clearly communicating what you paid for the vehicle, what your dealership needs to make to stay in business, and what value justifies the price you're asking.[96] This approach actually strengthens your negotiating position because customers who understand your costs and constraints become partners in finding mutually acceptable solutions rather than adversaries trying to extract maximum concessions.[91] [92 93]

Implementing Transparent Pricing in Practice

Start by showing customers the actual invoice when discussing pricing. Explain each component: the base vehicle cost, destination charges, any dealer-installed accessories, and applicable manufacturer incentives.[91 93 94] Be honest about holdback—the percentage manufacturers return to dealers after sale—and explain that this helps cover dealership operating costs like facility maintenance, staff salaries, and inventory financing.

When customers ask about your margin, give them a straightforward answer: "We need to make between $1,200 and $1,800 on this vehicle to cover our costs and stay profitable. That's significantly less than most people assume dealerships make." This honesty disarms the adversarial dynamic that traditional negotiation creates.[91 92 93] Research on negotiation consistently shows that transparency about constraints and interests leads to better outcomes for both parties than positional bargaining where each side guards information.

Present your pricing consistently across all platforms—your website, third-party listing sites, phone quotes, and in-person discussions.[92 94] Nothing destroys trust faster than a customer discovering that the price they saw online differs from what you're quoting in person. Use technology to your advantage: many dealerships now employ AI-driven pricing tools that adjust based on real-time market conditions, inventory age, and local demand, then display these prices transparently to customers both online and in the showroom.[95][97]

Communicating Value, Not Just Cost

Transparent pricing works best when paired with clear value communication. Don't just show customers what they're paying—show them what they're receiving. If your price is higher than a competitor's, explain specifically why: your lifetime powertrain warranty versus their limited coverage, your complimentary maintenance package, your loaner vehicle program during service, your customer loyalty benefits for future purchases.[96]

I learned this approach from a customer named Marcus who told me, "I can get this car for $800 less forty miles away. Convince me why I should pay more here." Instead of immediately discounting, I created a spreadsheet showing total cost of ownership over five years, including the services and benefits we provided that the other dealership charged extra for. The math showed our higher purchase price actually represented lower total cost.[96] Marcus appreciated the transparency and bought that day, later telling me, "You're the first salesperson who treated me like I was smart enough to understand the real numbers."

Transparent pricing isn't about being the cheapest—it's about being the most trustworthy.[91] When customers understand exactly what they're paying and why, they make confident decisions they feel good about long after the initial excitement fades.[91][92][93] That confidence transforms one-time buyers into lifelong advocates who generate the referrals and repeat business that sustainable careers are built on.[91][96]

Trade-In Negotiations That Preserve Relationships: Valuation Techniques That Customers Understand and Accept

Trade-in negotiations represent one of the most delicate moments in automotive sales—a point where trust can either solidify or shatter completely. I learned this lesson the hard way early in my career when a customer named Patricia walked away from what should have been an easy deal because she felt I'd undervalued her trade-in without adequate explanation. She didn't argue or get angry; she simply said, "I don't think you're being straight with me," and left. That moment taught me that how you handle trade-in valuation matters as much as the actual number you offer.

The traditional approach to trade-ins—treating them as negotiating leverage to manipulate overall deal structure—has created decades of customer distrust. Customers arrive expecting to be "lowballed" on their trade, anticipating that you'll use confusing math to hide profit in one area while appearing to give concessions in another. This adversarial expectation poisons negotiations before they begin. The relationship-preserving alternative requires a fundamental shift: treat the trade-in as a separate, transparent transaction that customers can understand and verify.[98][99][101]

Separating Trade-In from Purchase Negotiations

The single most important technique for preserving trust during trade-ins is separating the trade-in valuation from the new vehicle purchase.[98][99][101][102] When you blend these negotiations together, customers rightfully suspect that numbers are being manipulated to create the illusion of a good deal while obscuring actual costs and values.[101] I always establish the out-the-door price of the new vehicle first, ensuring the customer understands and accepts that number before we discuss their trade-in.[98][101] This separation eliminates confusion and demonstrates that you're not playing shell games with figures.

When a customer named David recently brought in his truck for trade, I walked him through this process explicitly: "Let's make sure we're on the same page about the new SUV first. Here's the price, here are the fees, here's your total cost. Once you're comfortable with that, we'll evaluate your trade completely separately. Fair?" David later told me this approach immediately reduced his defensiveness because he could evaluate each transaction on its own merits.

Transparent Valuation Using Market Data

Customers accept trade-in values they understand. Rather than simply announcing a number, walk them through your valuation process using the same tools they've likely already consulted—Kelley Blue Book, Edmunds, or similar resources.[99] Pull up these sites on your computer or tablet, enter their vehicle's details together, and review the trade-in range these sources provide. Explain how condition, mileage, local market demand, and any needed reconditioning affect where their specific vehicle falls within that range.[99]

I keep my tablet handy specifically for this purpose. When customers see you using the same objective data sources they trust, rather than mysterious "book values" they can't verify, resistance drops dramatically. One customer, Maria, arrived convinced we'd offer thousands below fair value. When I showed her the Edmunds trade-in estimate and explained that our offer of $14,200 fell within their "good condition" range of $13,800 to $14,600, accounting for the minor door ding and worn driver's seat, she nodded and said, "That's actually fair. I was expecting you to start at $11,000 and make me fight for every dollar."

Inviting Customer Participation in Appraisal

Transform the appraisal from something done to the customer into something done with them. Invite them to walk through the vehicle inspection with you, pointing out both positive attributes and issues that affect value. "Your maintenance records are excellent—that adds value. The tires have good tread remaining—that helps. This scratch on the bumper and the crack in the windshield will need repair before we can retail it, which affects what we can offer."[99]

This collaborative approach accomplishes two things: it demonstrates respect for the customer's intelligence, and it preempts objections by addressing condition issues openly rather than having them emerge as surprises when you present your offer.[98][100] Customers who participate in their vehicle's appraisal rarely dispute the resulting valuation because they've seen the reasoning firsthand.

Encouraging Competitive Quotes

Here's a technique that seems counterintuitive but builds tremendous trust: encourage customers to get trade-in quotes from multiple sources, including other dealerships and online buyers like Carvana or Vroom.[99][100][101] Tell them explicitly, "I want you to feel confident you're getting fair value. If you'd like to get quotes elsewhere for comparison, I completely understand and encourage it."

This recommendation demonstrates confidence in your valuation and eliminates the customer's suspicion that you're taking advantage of their lack of alternatives. When customers return with competitive quotes—which they often do—you can either match legitimate offers or explain specific reasons why another quote might be higher (perhaps they're not accounting for needed repairs, or they're using the vehicle to attract showroom traffic with no intention of honoring that price).

The goal isn't winning every trade-in negotiation—it's ensuring customers feel the process was fair, transparent, and respectful.[98] [99] [100] [101] When Patricia, the customer I lost years ago, recently returned to our dealership, she worked with me again specifically because another salesperson had recommended me, saying, "He'll be straight with you about your trade." That reputation, built through consistent transparency, has generated more long-term value than any individual deal I might have "won" through manipulation ever could.

Structuring Deals for Long-Term Satisfaction: Payment Options, Term Lengths, and Add-Ons That Customers Won't Regret

The moment when you transition from "which vehicle" to "how to structure the deal" represents a critical juncture where long-term satisfaction is either built or destroyed. I've seen countless salespeople celebrate closing deals with extended loan terms and maximum add-ons, only to watch those same customers return months later with buyer's remorse, negative equity, and zero intention of ever referring friends or returning for their next purchase. The deals that generate lasting satisfaction—and the referrals and repeat business that follow—are structured with the customer's long-term financial wellbeing as the priority, not just the immediate commission opportunity.

Payment Options That Serve Customer Needs

Today's customers typically choose between cash purchase, financing, or leasing, and your role is helping them understand which option genuinely serves their situation rather than which generates the highest dealership profit. Cash purchases eliminate interest costs entirely but require substantial available funds.[103] Financing—arranged either through the dealership or external lenders like banks and credit unions—allows customers to spread payments over time while building equity in the vehicle.[103][105][107] Leasing offers lower monthly payments for customers who prefer driving newer vehicles every few years without ownership.[103]

The ethical approach requires presenting all options transparently and encouraging customers to compare offers.[103][105][108] I always tell customers, "Get quotes from your bank or credit union before we finalize anything. I want you to have the best rate available, whether that's through us or elsewhere." This recommendation seems counterintuitive—why send customers to competitors?—but it builds trust that generates referrals worth far more than any single financing markup.

Credit unions often offer lower interest rates than dealership financing, though dealerships sometimes provide manufacturer incentives like 0% APR or special rebates that offset higher rates elsewhere.[105][106][107] The key is presenting the total cost comparison honestly: "Our rate is 5.9% versus your credit union's 4.2%, but we're offering a $2,000 manufacturer rebate that's only available with our financing. Let me show you the total cost of each option over the loan term so you can make an informed decision."[108]

Term Length: The Hidden Cost Multiplier

Loan term length dramatically affects both monthly payments and total cost, yet many customers focus exclusively on the monthly number without understanding the trade-off. A $35,000 loan at 9% APR with no down payment costs $727 monthly over 60 months with $8,593 in total interest, but extending to 84 months drops the payment to $563 while increasing total interest to $12,302—nearly $4,000 more for the convenience of lower monthly payments.[104]

I learned to present this visually after a customer named Steven returned eighteen months after his purchase, frustrated that he owed more than his vehicle was worth. He'd focused entirely on getting his payment under $400 monthly, accepting an 84-month term without understanding the implications. "You never explained I'd be upside down for years," he said, hurt evident in his voice. He was right—I'd presented the monthly payment he wanted without ensuring he understood the total cost and equity-building timeline.

Now I always show customers a comparison chart displaying monthly payment, total interest cost, and equity position at common trade-in intervals (36, 48, and 60 months) for different term lengths.[104 108] "Longer terms mean lower payments but significantly higher total cost and slower equity building.[104 106 108] If you typically trade vehicles every four to five years, an 84-month loan leaves you owing more than the vehicle's worth when you're ready to trade, which creates problems for your next purchase."[106]

Add-Ons That Enhance Rather Than Exploit

Extended warranties, maintenance packages, security systems, and accessories represent legitimate value when they address genuine customer concerns—and regrettable expenses when they're sold through pressure rather than need. The difference lies in consultative questioning: "What concerns you most about ownership costs?" rather than "Do you want the extended warranty?"

When a customer mentions worry about repair costs after warranty expiration, an extended warranty becomes a solution to a real concern.

When a customer expresses no such concern but you push the warranty anyway because it carries high commission, you've created future regret. I structure add-on conversations around the customer's actual situation: "You mentioned you keep vehicles for eight to ten years. The manufacturer warranty covers three years. Let me show you average repair costs for this model between years four and eight, and you can decide whether the extended coverage makes sense for your situation."[108]

The deals customers feel best about months and years later are those structured around their genuine needs and long-term financial health, not around maximizing immediate dealership profit. When you prioritize their satisfaction over your commission, something remarkable happens: they return, they refer others, and they tell everyone that you're different from every other car salesperson they've encountered. That reputation becomes the foundation of a sustainable career built on relationships rather than transactions.

Handling Competitive Quotes and Price Matching: Responding to Outside Offers Without Destroying Trust or Profit

The first time a customer walked into my dealership with three printed quotes from competitors, all neatly highlighted and organized in a folder, I felt my stomach tighten. My immediate instinct—shaped by years of traditional training—was defensive: dismiss the quotes as incomplete, question their legitimacy, or immediately offer to beat them by fifty dollars just to close the deal. I did none of those things, and that restraint taught me one of the most valuable lessons of my career.

Competitive quotes have become standard equipment for today's car buyers, as common as test drives once were.[110] Customers arrive with offers from online retailers, neighboring dealerships, and even out-of-state sellers willing to ship vehicles. This reality terrifies some salespeople who see each outside quote as a threat to their commission. But I've learned that competitive quotes represent something far more valuable: an opportunity to demonstrate the integrity and value that builds lasting relationships.

Verify Before You React

When a customer presents a competitive quote, your first response sets the tone for everything that follows. I always start with genuine curiosity rather than skepticism: "I appreciate you sharing this with me. Can I take a closer look so I can understand exactly what they're offering?" This simple request accomplishes two things—it shows respect for their research, and it gives you time to evaluate the offer properly.

Not all quotes are created equal.[109][100] Some exclude destination charges, dealer fees, or required add-ons. Others quote lease payments without disclosing money factor or residual value. I once had a customer show me a quote that appeared $1,200 lower than ours until we discovered it didn't include the destination charge or documentation fees—standard costs at every dealership. When I showed him the itemized comparison, he said, "I'm glad you caught that. I almost drove an hour based on incomplete information."

The key is presenting this information without sounding like you're making excuses. Pull up your computer screen, show the customer your detailed breakdown, and walk through each line item together.[109][100] Transparency here builds trust that pays dividends throughout the negotiation.[109][100]

Respond to Value, Not Just Price

The most common mistake I see salespeople make with competitive quotes is immediately offering to match or beat the price without discussing what differentiates the offers. Price matching might save the immediate sale, but it trains customers to see vehicles as commodities where only price matters—a race to the bottom that destroys profit margins and eliminates any reason for customers to return to you specifically.

Instead, I've learned to explore what's driving their decision beyond price: "I see their offer is lower. Before we talk about matching it, help me understand—if price were equal, what would make you choose to buy from us versus them?" This question reveals what they actually value: proximity to home, service department reputation, your personal rapport, financing options, or simply the confidence that comes from working with someone they trust.[109][100]

A customer named James once brought me a quote $800 lower from a dealership forty-five minutes away. Rather than immediately discounting, I asked about his priorities. He mentioned he'd bought his last two vehicles from us, always brought them here for service, and valued the relationship. I created a spreadsheet showing the total cost of ownership over five years, including our complimentary maintenance program, free loaner vehicles during service, and customer loyalty discount on his next purchase—benefits the other dealership didn't offer.[109][100] The math showed our higher purchase price actually represented lower total cost and greater convenience. James bought that day and later told me, "You helped me see past the sticker price to what actually matters."

When to Match, When to Walk

Sometimes competitive quotes are legitimate and comparable, requiring a decision: match the price or lose the sale. I've developed a framework for these moments that preserves both profit and relationship. If the customer has demonstrated genuine engagement—spent time with you, test-driven vehicles, asked thoughtful questions—and the competing offer is verifiable and comparable, matching or coming very close often makes sense.[109][100] You're investing in a relationship that can generate referrals and repeat business worth far more than the margin you're protecting on this single deal.[109][100]

However, if a customer is clearly using your time and expertise to validate a purchase they intend to make elsewhere, or if matching would require selling below your dealership's minimum acceptable margin, you need the confidence to let them walk.[109][100] I always do this gracefully: "I understand price is your primary consideration, and I respect that. Based on what you've shared, it sounds like the other dealership has the right offer for you. If anything changes or if I can help in the future, please don't hesitate to reach out." This response preserves dignity on both sides and occasionally brings customers back when they discover the cheaper option came with hidden compromises.

The goal isn't winning every price negotiation—it's building a reputation for fairness, transparency, and value that makes customers choose you even when you're not the absolute lowest price.[109][100] That reputation, earned through hundreds of honest interactions with competitive quotes, becomes your most powerful competitive advantage in a market where customers have infinite options and zero tolerance for manipulation.##

Conclusion: From Negotiation to Relationship

The negotiation techniques I've shared in this chapter represent more than tactical adjustments to how you discuss pricing, trade-ins, or payment structures—they represent a fundamental philosophical shift in how you understand your role in the automotive sales process. When I first entered this industry over two decades ago, negotiation was framed as a contest where skill meant extracting maximum profit while making customers feel they'd won something. The best negotiators, we were told, were those who could manipulate information, create pressure, and close deals that heavily favored the dealership regardless of how customers felt afterward.

That approach is dying, and for good reason. Today's digitally-informed customers arrive with pricing research, competitive quotes, and a healthy skepticism born from decades of industry reputation for adversarial tactics. They can verify your claims instantly on their smartphones, compare your offer against a dozen alternatives without leaving your showroom, and share their experience—positive or negative—with thousands of potential customers through online reviews and social media. In this environment, the negotiation strategies that worked through information asymmetry and pressure don't just fail—they actively destroy the trust and reputation that modern automotive careers are built upon.

The win-win framework, transparent pricing strategies, relationship-preserving trade-in techniques, long-term deal structuring, and authentic responses to competitive quotes I've outlined here share a common thread: they treat customers as intelligent partners in a collaborative problem-solving process rather than adversaries to overcome. This isn't about being "soft" on profit or accepting whatever customers demand—every technique in this chapter protects legitimate dealership margins while building customer satisfaction. The difference lies in how you achieve profitability: through manipulation and pressure that generates one-time transactions, or through transparency and value creation that generates loyal advocates.

The mathematics of relationship-based negotiation are compelling and undeniable. A customer who feels manipulated during negotiation might represent one sale and zero referrals—perhaps $2,000 in gross profit that ends the moment they drive away. A customer who experiences collaborative, transparent negotiation might generate three to five sales over their lifetime through repeat purchases and referrals—$8,000 to $12,000 in total gross profit, plus the immeasurable value of positive online reviews that attract new prospects already predisposed to trust you. When you view negotiation through this lens, the choice becomes obvious: short-term transactional victories or long-term relationship-based success.

I've watched this transformation play out across hundreds of negotiations over my career. The deals I'm proudest of aren't those where I extracted maximum profit through clever tactics—they're those where customers left feeling genuinely good about their decisions, returned for their next vehicle without shopping elsewhere, and sent friends and family with the simple recommendation: "Go see them. They'll treat you right." Those relationships, built one transparent negotiation at a time, have created a career that gets easier and more rewarding each year as reputation and referrals compound.

As you move forward, remember that every negotiation is an audition for a long-term relationship. The customer sitting across from you isn't just deciding whether to buy this vehicle at this dealership—they're deciding whether you're someone they can trust with future purchases, whether they'll recommend you to people they care about, and whether they'll share their experience publicly in ways that attract or repel future customers. Negotiate with that broader context in mind, and you'll discover that creating win-win outcomes isn't just the ethical approach—it's the foundation of sustainable success in modern automotive sales.

Chapter 7

Car Sales Closing Strategies: Ethical Techniques That Seal the Deal

T he moment of closing has been mythologized in automotive sales as a high-stakes confrontation where clever tactics overcome customer resistance and seal the deal through sheer force of will. But this dramatic narrative misses a fundamental truth: when the entire sales process has been built on trust, understanding, and genuine value creation, closing becomes less about pressure and more about helping a ready customer take the logical next step. The moment of closing has been mythologized in automotive sales as a high-stakes confrontation where clever tactics overcome customer resistance and seal the deal through sheer force of will. But this dramatic narrative misses a fundamental truth: when the entire sales process has been built on trust, understanding, and genuine value creation, closing becomes less about pressure and more about helping a ready customer take the logical next step.

For decades, the automotive industry celebrated closers who could deploy an arsenal of manipulative techniques—the "puppy dog close," the "take-away close," the "Ben Franklin close"—as if customers were puzzles to be solved through psychological tricks rather than people making significant financial decisions. These tactics generated short-term results but destroyed long-term relationships, leaving customers with buyer's remorse and sales professionals with reputations that made every subsequent interaction more difficult. In today's transparent, digitally-connected marketplace where a single negative review can reach thousands of potential customers, these outdated approaches don't just feel wrong—they're commercially destructive.

The evolution toward ethical closing strategies represents more than a moral improvement; it reflects a fundamental market shift. Modern car buyers arrive at dealerships having completed extensive online research, read countless reviews, and often pre-qualified for financing. They're not uninformed prospects waiting to be convinced—they're educated consumers looking for confirmation that their research led them to the right decision and the right dealership. The closing techniques that work with these customers facilitate decision-making rather than manufacture it, address legitimate final concerns rather than manufacture urgency, and create confidence that lasts long after the paperwork is signed.

This chapter will equip you with closing strategies that honor customer intelligence while recognizing a simple reality: even satisfied, ready-to-buy customers sometimes need help taking that final step. You'll learn to recognize genuine buying signals that indicate readiness versus polite disengagement that suggests unresolved concerns. You'll discover how to use assumptive language and trial closes throughout the sales process—not as manipulation tactics, but as collaborative temperature checks that keep you aligned with customer readiness. Most importantly, you'll master the art of addressing final hesitations authentically, distinguishing between last-minute concerns that deserve exploration and exit strategies that require graceful acceptance.

The techniques you'll encounter here come from real dealership floors where relationship-focused sales professionals consistently outperform their high-pressure colleagues—not just in immediate sales volume, but in customer satisfaction scores, referral generation, and repeat business that compounds over time. You'll see how ethical closing creates customers who feel empowered by their decisions rather than pressured into them, generating the positive reviews and enthusiastic referrals that make future closes easier because trust precedes the first conversation. Whether you're transitioning from another industry or refining your existing approach, these strategies will show you that closing isn't about winning a negotiation—it's about confidently guiding a ready customer across the finish line of a decision they already want to make.

Recognizing Genuine Buying Signals: How to Know When Customers Are Ready Without Guessing or Pushing Prematurely

I learned the hard way that pushing for a close before a customer is ready doesn't just kill the current sale—it destroys any chance of a future relationship. Early in my career, I mistook a customer's polite engagement for buying intent and launched into closing mode while he was still gathering information. His body language shifted immediately from open to defensive, and he left within minutes. That experience taught me something crucial: recognizing genuine buying signals isn't about guessing or hoping—it's about observing specific, measurable behaviors that indicate readiness.

Genuine buying signals fall into three distinct categories, and understanding each helps you engage at precisely the right moment without premature pressure. The first category is **verbal signals** —the questions customers ask when they've mentally shifted from "if" to "when."[113][115] Listen for inquiries about delivery timelines: "How soon could I take delivery?"[115] or financing specifics: "What would my monthly payment look like?"[112][115] These questions reveal that customers are visualizing ownership rather than gathering general information.[113][115] When someone asks about warranty coverage, trade-in procedures, or after-sales service[115], they're no longer browsing—they're evaluating the practical logistics of a decision they're preparing to make.

The second category involves **behavioral and non-verbal signals** that often speak louder than words. Watch for customers who return multiple times to the same vehicle, linger during test drives, or bring family members or partners to subsequent visits.[113][115] Physical engagement matters: when customers start touching surfaces, adjusting seats, or opening compartments repeatedly[115], they're mentally taking ownership. Body language shifts are equally telling—leaning forward during conversations, maintaining sustained eye contact, nodding in agreement, or displaying open, relaxed postures all indicate receptiveness.[115][116] I've found that customers who introduce decision-makers into the process— "I'd like my wife to see this before we decide"—are signaling serious intent, not creating obstacles.[113]

The third category reflects our digital reality: **online and service-related signals** that precede showroom visits. Customers who schedule test drives through your website[112], request personalized quotes via email, or repeatedly visit specific vehicle pages on your dealership site[114] are demonstrating high purchase intent. According to Cox Automotive research, dealerships that leverage CRM data to identify these digital behaviors and proactively reach out see significantly higher conversion rates.[111] One particularly valuable signal comes from your service department: customers bringing vehicles in for costly repairs, especially those with positive equity, often represent prime opportunities for trade-up conversations—not through pressure, but through helpful information about their options.[111]

The critical skill lies in distinguishing genuine signals from casual interest. Genuine buyers engage deeper and more persistently—they ask specific, actionable questions, compare your offerings to competitors, and demonstrate sustained attention across multiple interactions.[113][115] Casual browsers ask general questions, show brief engagement, and lack follow-through on concrete next steps like test drives or price discussions.[115]

Research from sales analytics firm Attention.com found that early detection of buying signals can increase conversion rates by up to thirty percent[113], but only when sales professionals respond appropriately. The key word is "respond," not "pounce." When you recognize genuine buying signals, your role shifts from information provider to decision facilitator. Instead of deploying closing pressure, ask open-ended questions that help customers articulate their readiness: "It sounds like this vehicle checks all your boxes—what questions do you still have?" or "Based on what you've shared, does this feel like the right fit for your needs?"

The most successful approach treats buying signals as invitations to assist rather than triggers for aggressive closing.[115] When customers demonstrate readiness through multiple signals—asking about financing while physically engaging with the vehicle and mentioning their current car's problems—they're not playing hard to get. They're genuinely ready and simply need your confident guidance to take the next logical step. That's when ethical closing becomes natural, effective, and the foundation of relationships that generate referrals long after the sale concludes.

The Assumptive Close Done Right: Facilitating Natural Forward Movement Without Manipulation

The assumptive close gets a bad reputation because it's been misused for decades by salespeople who deployed it prematurely, before trust was established or concerns were addressed.[117] [118] But when executed properly—after you've listened deeply, resolved objections, and confirmed genuine readiness—the assumptive close isn't manipulation.[117] [118] [119] It's confident guidance that helps customers take the natural next step they're already prepared to make.

I remember working with a customer named Rachel who'd spent three visits with me over two weeks, test-driving a compact SUV, discussing financing options, and bringing her husband for his input. During our third meeting, after we'd addressed every concern and reviewed the numbers she'd agreed were fair, Rachel sat quietly at my desk, nodding slowly. Everything pointed to readiness—her verbal signals, her body language, her sustained engagement—but she seemed stuck in that final moment of hesitation that even confident buyers experience before major purchases.

Instead of asking "So, would you like to move forward?" which invited doubt and reopened the entire decision, I used assumptive language that acknowledged her readiness: "Let's get your paperwork started so you can take it home this weekend. Would Friday afternoon or Saturday morning work better for delivery?"[117] [118] Rachel's shoulders visibly relaxed. "Saturday morning would be perfect," she said, and we proceeded smoothly to completion. Months later, she told me that my confidence in that moment helped her move past the natural anxiety of a significant purchase. "You didn't pressure me," she explained. "You just acted like we were doing what we'd already decided to do, which we were."[117] [119]

That's the essence of the ethical assumptive close: using forward-moving language that treats the purchase as the logical conclusion of everything that's come before.[117][118] Instead of "Are you ready to buy?" you say "Let's talk about delivery timing." Instead of "Do you want to proceed?" you ask "Should we start with the paperwork or would you like one more test drive first?" These phrases assume positive intent while still offering the customer control and the opportunity to voice any remaining concerns.

The key distinction between ethical and manipulative assumptive closing lies entirely in timing and foundation. The manipulative version deploys assumptive language prematurely—before objections are resolved, before trust is established, before the customer is genuinely ready.[117][118] It attempts to manufacture momentum where none exists. The ethical version recognizes existing momentum and simply facilitates its natural progression.[117][118] You're not creating the decision; you're helping a ready customer execute a decision they've already made mentally.

This approach works particularly well when combined with what I call "choice-based assumptions" that give customers agency within the forward movement. "Would you prefer the extended warranty or the standard coverage?" assumes they're purchasing while letting them control the specifics.[117] "Should we schedule your first service appointment now or would you rather call later?" moves past the purchase decision to post-ownership logistics, reinforcing their mental shift to owner rather than shopper.[118]

The assumptive close also addresses a psychological reality: even satisfied customers sometimes need permission to stop deliberating and commit. Decision fatigue is real, especially for major purchases involving extensive research and multiple options.[118] When you've genuinely earned trust and addressed concerns, your confident assumption that they're ready can actually relieve anxiety rather than create it. You're essentially saying "Based on everything we've discussed, this is clearly the right decision for you"—and if you've done your job properly throughout the sales process, that statement is objectively true.

Watch carefully for the customer's response to your assumptive language. Genuine readiness produces relief and forward engagement: they answer your delivery-timing question, they discuss paperwork logistics, they ask about next steps.[118] Premature assumption produces hesitation, backtracking, or the reintroduction of concerns you thought were resolved.[117] [118] If you encounter the latter, you haven't failed—you've simply discovered that more conversation is needed. Gracefully shift back to exploration: "It sounds like something's still on your mind. What questions do you have?"[117]

The assumptive close done right transforms what could be an awkward, high-pressure moment into a natural transition that honors the customer's intelligence, respects their readiness, and demonstrates your confidence in the value you've provided throughout the entire process.[117] [118] [119]

Trial Closes and Temperature Checks: Collaborative Techniques for Gauging Customer Readiness Throughout the Process

The most valuable closing technique isn't actually a close at all—it's a series of collaborative checkpoints throughout the sales process that keep you aligned with your customer's readiness and concerns. I learned this lesson during my third year on the showroom floor when I watched a veteran salesperson named Marcus work with a hesitant couple. Instead of building toward one dramatic closing moment, he asked simple questions every few minutes: "How does this feature sound for your situation?" and "Is this heading in the right direction for you?" By the time they reached his desk to discuss numbers, closing was effortless because he'd been gauging and adjusting throughout their entire journey together.

Trial closes are low-pressure questions or statements woven naturally into conversation that invite customers to express opinions, reveal concerns, or indicate interest without committing to purchase.[16] Think of them as collaborative temperature checks that provide real-time feedback about where customers stand emotionally and practically. When you ask "How do you feel about the cargo space for your weekend camping trips?" during a test drive, you're not pushing for a sale—you're creating an opening for honest dialogue that helps you understand whether you're on the right track or need to adjust your approach.

The beauty of trial closes lies in their versatility and timing. You can deploy them during the vehicle walk-around ("Can you see yourself using this feature regularly?"), throughout the test drive ("How does this compare to what you've been driving?"), and while reviewing options ("Would this technology package add value for your daily commute?"). Each question serves dual purposes: it engages customers in evaluating fit while simultaneously revealing objections, hesitations, or enthusiasm you might otherwise miss until it's too late to address them effectively.[16]

The most effective trial closes use open-ended phrasing that invites genuine response rather than yes-or-no answers that customers can deflect. Instead of "Do you like this color?" try "How does this color work with your preferences?" The subtle difference creates space for customers to share authentic reactions—"Actually, I was hoping for something darker" gives you actionable information, while a polite "It's fine" tells you nothing and masks potential concerns that will surface later as objections.

Temperature checks take this concept further by directly assessing customer comfort and confidence at strategic moments.[16] I regularly use phrases like "On a scale of one to ten, how close does this feel to what you're looking for?" or "What questions are still on your mind as we move forward?" These aren't manipulative tactics—they're respectful acknowledgments that buying a vehicle is a significant decision deserving of careful consideration and ongoing dialogue.

The collaborative nature of these techniques transforms your role from persuader to partner.[16] When a customer responds to your temperature check with "I'm at about a seven—I'm still concerned about the monthly payment," you've just received an invitation to solve a specific problem rather than guessing what's holding them back. This transparency prevents the awkward scenario where you present final numbers only to discover a deal-breaking concern that could have been addressed hours earlier.

Research in sales psychology consistently shows that customers who feel heard and understood throughout the process experience significantly less buyer's remorse and generate more referrals than those pushed through a linear sales script.[16] Trial closes and temperature checks operationalize this principle, creating multiple opportunities for customers to voice concerns, ask questions, and confirm alignment before reaching the final commitment stage.

The key is authenticity—these techniques only work when you genuinely care about the answers and respond collaboratively to what you hear.[16] If a customer expresses hesitation during a trial close, don't dismiss it or immediately counter with more selling. Instead, explore it: "Tell me more about that concern. Let's make sure we address it fully." That response builds trust and positions you as someone working with them rather than against their natural caution, making the eventual close feel like a natural conclusion rather than a high-pressure moment they've been dreading.

Addressing Final Hesitations: Distinguishing Between Last-Minute Concerns and Polite Exit Strategies

The most delicate moment in any automotive sale arrives when a customer pauses, shifts their weight slightly, and says something that could mean everything or nothing: "I need to think about it." In that instant, you face a critical choice that will define not just this transaction, but your entire relationship with this person. Are they expressing a genuine concern that deserves exploration, or are they politely signaling that something fundamental isn't right and they need an exit?[117][121]

I learned to distinguish between these scenarios the hard way. Early in my career, I treated every hesitation as an objection to overcome, deploying the closing techniques I'd been taught without considering what customers were actually communicating. A woman named Sandra spent two hours with me, engaged throughout, asked thoughtful questions, and seemed genuinely interested in a sedan we'd discussed. When she said "I need to talk to my husband," I launched into a scripted response about decision-making authority, essentially suggesting she didn't need his input. Her expression changed immediately—not to agreement, but to something between offense and discomfort. She left within minutes and never returned. I'd mistaken a legitimate concern for a brush-off and responded with pressure when I should have offered support.

Genuine last-minute concerns have distinct characteristics that separate them from polite exits. Real concerns are specific and actionable: "I'm worried about the reliability record of this model year" or "I need to understand the warranty coverage better before committing."[117][121] These statements invite dialogue and problem-solving. The customer's body language remains engaged—they maintain eye contact, lean forward, and demonstrate openness to continued conversation.[117] Most tellingly, they ask questions that assume potential ownership: "What happens if I need service while traveling?" or "Can I add my daughter to the insurance before delivery?"

Polite exit strategies, by contrast, are deliberately vague and non-specific. "I'm just not sure right now" or "I want to sleep on it" without articulating what specifically needs consideration.[119][121] The body language shifts—customers begin gathering their belongings, checking their phones, moving toward the door, or breaking eye contact.[117] Their responses become shorter, less detailed, and increasingly noncommittal. When you ask clarifying questions, they deflect rather than engage: "I just need time" without explaining what they'll be thinking about during that time.

The ethical response to genuine concerns is straightforward: **explore them collaboratively without defensiveness.** When a customer expresses specific hesitation, respond with curiosity rather than rebuttal. "Tell me more about your reliability concerns—what would help you feel confident about that?"[121][122] This approach honors their intelligence and positions you as a partner in their decision-making rather than an adversary trying to overcome resistance. If they're worried about monthly payments, explore restructuring options together. If they're uncertain about a feature, offer additional demonstration or information from current owners. Genuine concerns, when addressed authentically, often strengthen rather than weaken the relationship because customers see that you're willing to work through obstacles rather than dismiss them.[117]

Recognizing polite exits requires both observation and respect. When multiple signals indicate disengagement—vague language, closed body language, deflection of specific questions—the ethical response is graceful acceptance, not increased pressure.[119][120] I now say something like: "I appreciate you taking the time to explore this with me. It sounds like this might not be the right fit or the right timing, and that's completely okay. Here's my card—if circumstances change or if I can answer questions down the road, please don't hesitate to reach out."[119][120] This response accomplishes something crucial: it preserves dignity and leaves the door open for future contact without making the customer feel trapped or pressured.[117]

The distinction matters profoundly because **misreading the situation damages trust irreparably.**[120][43] Pressuring someone who's genuinely ready but has one remaining concern can help facilitate a mutually beneficial sale. Pressuring someone who's signaling exit destroys any possibility of future relationship and often generates negative reviews that affect your reputation with prospects you haven't even met yet.[120][43] The sales professionals who build sustainable careers learn to read these signals accurately and respond with the customer's comfort as the priority, understanding that some of the best long-term relationships begin with respectfully letting someone walk away.[117][119][120][121]

Creating Post-Close Confidence: Ensuring Customers Feel Empowered About Their Decision Long After Signing

The sale doesn't end when the customer signs—it either begins a relationship or confirms their worst fears about car buying. I learned this during my second year on the showroom floor when a customer named Kevin returned three days after purchasing a truck, visibly anxious. "Did I make a mistake?" he asked. "I keep second-guessing the payment, wondering if I should have bought used instead." His question wasn't about the vehicle—it was about needing reassurance that his decision was sound. That conversation taught me something crucial: post-close confidence isn't automatic, even when customers are genuinely satisfied. It requires intentional reinforcement that transforms buyer's anxiety into buyer's pride.

Buyer's remorse is a psychological reality, not a character flaw. Research in consumer behavior consistently shows that major purchases trigger cognitive dissonance—the uncomfortable tension between the excitement of acquisition and the anxiety of commitment. For automotive purchases, this dissonance intensifies because customers are making their second-largest financial decision while navigating an industry with a reputation for manipulation. Your role in the hours, days, and weeks following the sale is to provide the emotional reassurance and logical validation that tips the balance toward confidence.[118]

The foundation of post-close confidence begins before the customer leaves your dealership. **The delivery experience sets the tone for everything that follows.** I make it standard practice to walk customers through their new vehicle systematically, demonstrating features they'll use regularly and ensuring they're comfortable with technology that might initially seem overwhelming.[118] This isn't just customer service—it's confidence building. When customers understand how to operate their vehicle's systems, they feel competent and in control rather than intimidated and regretful.

Equally important is **introducing customers to your service team personally.**[124] Walk them to the service department, introduce them by name to the service advisor, and explain how to schedule appointments.[124] This simple gesture transforms an abstract "dealership relationship" into concrete human connections. When Kevin returned with his concerns, I walked him back to meet our service manager, who spent fifteen minutes discussing the truck's maintenance schedule and reliability record. Kevin left reassured—not because I'd convinced him, but because he'd met another person invested in his satisfaction.[124]

Strategic follow-up communication reinforces confidence without feeling intrusive.[124][126] I send a personalized text twenty-four hours after delivery: "How's the first day with your new vehicle? Any questions about features?" This isn't a sales check-in—it's genuine support during the vulnerable period when doubts typically surface. Three days later, I follow with a brief call addressing common post-purchase concerns proactively: "I wanted to check in and remind you that it's completely normal to second-guess a major decision like this. But based on everything we discussed about your needs, this vehicle genuinely is the right fit. How are you feeling about it?"

The language matters enormously. Notice I acknowledged the normalcy of doubt rather than dismissing it, then connected back to their specific needs and priorities.[123] This approach validates their emotions[123] while reinforcing the logical foundation of their decision—addressing both the emotional and practical dimensions that drive automotive purchases.[118]

Digital touchpoints extend your post-close support beyond phone calls. I send new owners a welcome email within forty-eight hours containing helpful resources: tutorial videos for their vehicle's technology, maintenance schedules, and my direct contact information with explicit permission to reach out anytime.[124] I've also created a private Facebook group for my customers where they share experiences, ask questions, and support each other. This community reinforces their confidence through peer validation—seeing other satisfied owners enjoying the same vehicle they purchased.[123]

The most powerful post-close confidence builder is **demonstrating that your commitment extends beyond commission.**[125] When customers contact me months after their purchase with questions unrelated to future sales—"Can you recommend a good detailer?" or "What tire pressure should I use in winter?"—I respond promptly and helpfully. These micro-interactions prove that I view them as relationships, not transactions, which retrospectively validates their decision to buy from me rather than a competitor offering a slightly lower price.

Kevin became one of my most enthusiastic referral sources, sending four friends over two years. Each one mentioned the same thing during our first conversation: "Kevin said you actually care what happens after the sale." That reputation—built through intentional post-close confidence strategies—became my most valuable competitive advantage, generating sustainable success through loyalty rather than constantly chasing new prospects who arrive skeptical and leave uncertain. The closing moment reveals everything about who you are as a sales professional. After two decades on dealership floors, I've watched countless salespeople sabotage otherwise excellent sales processes by reverting to pressure tactics in those final minutes, as if all the trust-building that preceded it suddenly didn't matter. But I've also witnessed the quiet power of ethical closing—that moment when a customer visibly relaxes because your confidence helps them move past natural hesitation toward a decision they genuinely feel good about, not just today but months and years later when they're deciding whether to refer friends or return for their next vehicle.

The techniques in this chapter share a common foundation: they work *with* customer psychology rather than against it. Recognizing genuine buying signals prevents you from pushing prematurely and destroying rapport you've carefully built. The assumptive close, when deployed after trust is established and concerns are resolved, facilitates natural forward movement rather than manufacturing false urgency. Trial closes and temperature checks throughout the process keep you aligned with customer readiness, preventing that awkward moment where you discover deal-breaking concerns only after presenting final numbers. And distinguishing between genuine hesitations and polite exits ensures you address real concerns collaboratively while respecting when customers need space rather than pressure.

What separates ethical closing from manipulative tactics isn't just technique—it's intent and timing. Every strategy in this chapter assumes you've done the foundational work explored in previous chapters: understanding customer psychology, building genuine rapport, adapting to digitally-informed buyers, handling objections authentically, and negotiating for win-win outcomes. Closing isn't a standalone skill you deploy in isolation; it's the natural culmination of a consultative process where you've earned the right to guide confidently because you've genuinely served the customer's interests throughout their journey.

The post-close confidence strategies matter just as much as the close itself. Buyer's remorse isn't a sign that customers made wrong decisions—it's a psychological reality of major purchases that you can either ignore and hope resolves itself, or address proactively through thoughtful delivery experiences, strategic follow-up, and demonstrated commitment that extends beyond your commission. The customers who receive this support don't just feel better about their purchases; they become advocates who generate the referrals and repeat business that make future closes easier because trust precedes the first conversation.

I've built my career on a simple principle that this chapter reinforces: closing isn't about winning a negotiation or overcoming resistance through clever tactics. It's about confidently helping ready customers take the logical next step in a decision they want to make, then ensuring they feel empowered about that decision long after the initial excitement fades. The sales professionals who understand this distinction don't just close more deals—they build sustainable careers on relationships that compound over time, where satisfied customers become enthusiastic advocates and closing becomes progressively easier because reputation replaces skepticism.

The closing strategies that create one-time transactions through pressure might generate immediate results, but the techniques that honor customer intelligence and autonomy generate something far more valuable: loyalty, referrals, and a reputation that transforms you from just another car salesperson into a trusted advisor customers actively seek out and enthusiastically recommend to everyone they know.

Chapter 8

Car Dealership Success: Building Long-Term Relationships and Thriving in Digital Automotive Sales

Eliza stood in the dealership showroom on a quiet Tuesday morning, scrolling through her phone and smiling at a notification that had just appeared—a five-star Google review from a customer she'd worked with three years earlier, now thanking her for the exceptional service experience he'd just received. This moment captured the essence of modern automotive sales success: a relationship built years ago, maintained through consistent digital and personal touchpoints, generating ongoing value that extended far beyond the initial transaction. Eliza stood in the dealership showroom on a quiet Tuesday morning, scrolling through her phone and smiling at a notification that had just appeared—a five-star Google review from a customer she'd worked with three years earlier, now thanking her for the exceptional service experience he'd just received. This moment captured the essence of modern automotive sales success: a relationship built years ago, maintained through consistent digital and personal touchpoints, generating ongoing value that extended far beyond the initial transaction. That review represented something far more valuable than any single sale—it was evidence of a business model built on loyalty, systematic relationship maintenance, and the integration of digital tools with genuine human connection.

Throughout this book, we've traced the evolution of automotive sales from high-pressure tactics to relationship-driven approaches, explored the psychology that drives purchase decisions, learned to build authentic trust with skeptical customers, adapted to the digitally-informed buyer, transformed objections into opportunities, created win-win negotiations, and mastered ethical closing techniques. Now, in this final chapter, we bring all these elements together to show you how to build sustainable dealership success that thrives in today's hybrid marketplace where digital research and in-person relationships intersect.

The automotive sales professionals who succeed long-term understand a fundamental truth: your career isn't built on the number of vehicles you sell this month—it's built on the strength of relationships that generate repeat business, referrals, and reputation years into the future. While your colleagues chase new prospects through expensive advertising and cold outreach, you'll discover how to create a self-sustaining business where satisfied customers become your most effective marketing force, where your digital presence works for you around the clock, and where each relationship you build makes the next sale easier because trust precedes you.

This chapter provides the comprehensive framework for creating customer lifetime value through systematic relationship maintenance integrated with smart digital presence management. You'll learn specific strategies for staying connected with customers long after delivery without being intrusive, leveraging social media and online reviews authentically to build your professional brand, implementing omnichannel communication that meets customers where they are, and using CRM systems and technology to enhance rather than replace human connection. Whether you're an individual sales professional building your personal book of business or a manager developing dealership-wide strategies, these approaches will show you how to create stability and growth regardless of market conditions, inventory challenges, or competitive pressures.

The story you're about to read follows Eliza's journey from real estate to automotive sales, where she applied relationship-building principles that initially puzzled her colleagues but ultimately transformed not just her own success, but her entire dealership's approach to customer relationships and digital integration. Her experience demonstrates that modern dealership success isn't about working harder to find more prospects—it's about working smarter to create more value from the customers you already have, building a reputation-based business that compounds over time rather than starting from zero each month.

The Customer Lifetime Value Mindset: Why Long-Term Relationships Generate More Profit Than Transaction-Focused Selling

Three years after Daniel's initial purchase, Eliza watched her monthly commission statement with a sense of satisfaction that had nothing to do with a single big sale. While her colleague Marcus celebrated closing five deals that week—his best performance in months—Eliza's income came from a different source entirely: two repeat customers returning for their next vehicles, three referrals from satisfied clients, and a steady stream of service appointments she'd facilitated that earned her bonuses through the dealership's relationship incentive program.[14][15]

Marcus had worked sixty-hour weeks cold-calling prospects and greeting every walk-in with aggressive enthusiasm. Eliza had worked forty hours, spent Tuesday afternoon at her daughter's school event, and still out-earned him by eighteen percent. The difference wasn't talent or effort—it was understanding a fundamental economic principle that transforms how successful salespeople approach their careers.

The Mathematics of Lifetime Value

When Eliza transitioned from real estate to automotive sales, she brought a crucial insight: the average car buyer purchases approximately thirteen vehicles over their lifetime. If you sell someone one car and never see them again, you've captured one-thirteenth of their potential value. But if you maintain that relationship, you've positioned yourself to capture not just their future purchases, but their family members' purchases and their referrals' purchases as well.

The numbers tell a compelling story. Industry data shows that acquiring a new customer costs dealerships five to seven times more than retaining an existing one through marketing, advertising, and sales effort. Yet the traditional automotive sales model treats each transaction as isolated—celebrate the close, move to the next prospect, repeat. This approach leaves enormous value uncaptured.

Consider Daniel's relationship with Eliza over those three years. His initial sedan purchase generated a $3,200 commission. But the lifetime value of that relationship included his wife's subsequent SUV purchase ($2,800 commission), four referrals who purchased vehicles ($11,400 in total commissions), and service department bonuses totaling $640 as Daniel returned consistently for maintenance. That single relationship generated $18,040 over three years—nearly six times the initial transaction value.

Why Relationships Compound While Transactions Don't

The transaction-focused salesperson starts each month at zero, hunting for new prospects to hit quota. The relationship-focused salesperson starts each month with a foundation of past customers who generate repeat business, referrals, and advocacy without additional acquisition cost.[14][15]

This compounding effect accelerates over time. In your first year, you're building your customer base from scratch. By year three, if you've maintained relationships systematically, thirty to forty percent of your business comes from repeat and referral sources. By year five, that percentage can exceed sixty percent—meaning the majority of your income requires no cold prospecting, no advertising spend, no starting from zero with skeptical strangers.

I learned this principle the hard way during my second year in the business. I'd had a phenomenal month closing twelve deals—my personal best. I celebrated, took my foot off the relationship-maintenance pedal, and focused entirely on new prospects the following month. Three months later, my income crashed because I'd neglected follow-up with previous customers. Two of them purchased vehicles from competitors. One specifically told me later, "I didn't hear from you after I bought, so I figured you didn't care about my business anymore."

That painful lesson taught me that every customer represents a choice: treat them as a transaction that ends at delivery, or as a relationship that begins there. The former generates one-time revenue. The latter generates compounding returns that build sustainable careers.

The Trust Dividend

Beyond pure economics, long-term relationships create something transaction-focused selling cannot: trust that precedes you. When Maria contacted Eliza through Daniel's referral, she arrived pre-sold on Eliza's integrity. The typical barriers—skepticism, defensiveness, price-grinding—simply didn't exist. Maria's purchase process took half the time and generated higher customer satisfaction scores because trust had been transferred through the relationship.[14][17]

This "trust dividend" transforms your daily work. Instead of convincing skeptical strangers, you're helping referred customers who already believe you'll treat them fairly.[16] Instead of overcoming objections rooted in industry-wide distrust, you're addressing legitimate questions from people who assume your intentions are good. The emotional labor of selling decreases dramatically while effectiveness increases.

The customer lifetime value mindset isn't about manipulation or extracting maximum profit from relationships—it's about recognizing that when you genuinely serve customers well, maintain consistent contact, and prioritize their long-term satisfaction over short-term commission, you create economic value that far exceeds any individual transaction.[14][15] The salespeople who understand this don't just earn more—they build careers they actually enjoy, working with people who trust them rather than constantly battling skepticism in an endless hunt for the next deal.[14][15][17]

Digital Presence Management: Building Your Professional Brand Through Social Media, Reviews, and Online Reputation

Six months into her automotive sales career, Eliza made a discovery that would fundamentally change her approach to building business: a potential customer named Rachel had found her through a Google search, read through seventeen of her online reviews, watched three videos she'd posted on Instagram showing vehicle features, and arrived at the dealership already convinced she wanted to work with Eliza specifically. The entire sales process took ninety minutes because trust had been established digitally before they ever met in person.

This experience crystallized a truth that many veteran salespeople still resist: your digital presence isn't separate from your sales career—it is your sales career's foundation in the modern marketplace.[14] While your physical presence matters during the hours you're on the showroom floor, your digital presence works for you twenty-four hours a day, seven days a week, building credibility, answering questions, and pre-qualifying prospects who arrive ready to buy because they've already decided you're someone they can trust.[14][15]

Your Social Media Strategy: Authenticity Over Volume

The most common mistake salespeople make with social media is treating it like a digital billboard—constant inventory posts, sales announcements, and promotional content that screams "I want your business" without offering any genuine value. Rachel later told Eliza that she'd looked at three other salespeople's social media profiles before choosing her. "Two of them just posted car after car with prices," Rachel explained. "The third barely posted at all. But your Instagram actually taught me things I didn't know about features I was researching. You felt like someone who could help me, not just sell to me."

Eliza's approach was deliberately different. She posted twice weekly: one educational piece addressing common customer questions (how to use advanced safety features, what to look for during test drives, seasonal maintenance tips) and one personal connection piece (customer delivery photos with permission, community involvement, behind-the-scenes dealership moments that humanized her work). She never posted pricing or aggressive sales pitches. Instead, she positioned herself as a helpful resource who happened to sell cars rather than a salesperson desperately seeking attention.

This strategy generated measurable results. Over eighteen months, Eliza tracked that twenty-three customers specifically mentioned finding her through social media, and her content was shared forty-seven times by customers who found it genuinely useful.[14] The key wasn't posting frequency or follower count—it was consistent value creation that built her reputation as knowledgeable, trustworthy, and customer-focused.[14 15]

Online Reviews: Your Most Powerful Marketing Asset

When I started in automotive sales, online reviews barely existed. Today, they're often the first—and sometimes only—impression potential customers form before deciding whether to contact you. Research consistently shows that consumers trust online reviews nearly as much as personal recommendations, and the presence of reviews (even some negative ones) builds more credibility than having no reviews at all.[14]

Eliza developed a simple but effective review generation system. Three days after delivery, she sent a personalized text: "How's everything going with your new vehicle? Any questions I can help with?" This wasn't about the review—it was genuine follow-up.[14 15] But a week later, if the customer expressed satisfaction, she'd add: "I'm so glad you're happy! If you'd feel comfortable sharing your experience in a Google review, it really helps other people find me. No pressure either way—I'm just grateful for your business."

The magic was in the authenticity and timing. She never asked for reviews immediately after delivery when customers were still in the emotional high of a new purchase. She waited until they'd lived with the vehicle, experienced her follow-up support, and could provide genuine feedback. Her review request felt like an invitation rather than a demand, and her response rate exceeded forty percent—far above the industry average of fifteen to twenty percent.

Equally important was how Eliza responded to reviews. Every positive review received a personalized thank-you mentioning specific details from their experience. The three negative reviews she received over two years each got immediate, empathetic responses acknowledging the concern, offering to resolve the issue offline, and demonstrating to future readers that she took customer satisfaction seriously even when things went wrong.[14]

Managing Your Digital Reputation Proactively

Your online reputation isn't just what you post—it's everything the internet says about you. Eliza set up Google Alerts for her name and dealership, checked review platforms weekly, and maintained updated profiles on dealer rating sites. When a customer posted a complaint on Facebook about a service experience, Eliza saw it within hours, contacted the service department to investigate, and reached out to the customer directly to resolve the issue. That proactive response turned a potential reputation crisis into a demonstration of her commitment to customer care.[14][15]

The lesson Rachel's experience taught Eliza—and that I've seen validated across hundreds of successful salespeople—is that digital presence management isn't about self-promotion or manipulation. It's about making it easy for people researching you online to discover that you're knowledgeable, trustworthy, and genuinely committed to helping customers make good decisions.[14] [15] When your digital presence authentically reflects those qualities, prospects arrive pre-sold on working with you, transforming the sales process from convincing skeptics to serving people who already believe you'll treat them right.[16]

Omnichannel Communication Strategies: Seamlessly Integrating Phone, Text, Email, Social Media, and In-Person Touchpoints

When Marcus texted Eliza at 9:47 PM on a Thursday asking about a vehicle feature he couldn't figure out, she responded within twelve minutes with a helpful video link. The next morning, Marcus called the dealership to thank her, mentioning he'd also seen her response to his question in her Facebook group where another customer had chimed in with additional tips. That afternoon, he stopped by in person to finalize paperwork for his wife's vehicle purchase—a sale that had progressed seamlessly across four different communication channels without Marcus ever feeling like he was starting over or repeating information.

This experience illustrates what omnichannel communication actually means in practice: not just being available on multiple platforms, but creating a unified experience where customers can switch between channels fluidly while you maintain context and continuity.[127 128 132] The dealerships that master this integration don't just respond faster—they build relationships that feel effortless from the customer's perspective because every touchpoint connects to a complete understanding of their journey.[127 128]

Meeting Customers Where They Are

The fundamental principle of omnichannel communication is simple: different customers prefer different channels at different stages of their journey, and your job is to accommodate those preferences rather than forcing everyone into your preferred method.[129][130] Some customers want to text quick questions during their lunch break. Others prefer detailed email exchanges they can reference later. Some need phone conversations for complex financial discussions.[127][129][130] Many use social media to research your reputation before ever contacting you directly.[127][128][131]

I learned this lesson when I lost a sale early in my career by insisting a customer call me to discuss details he'd asked about via email. He wanted written information he could review with his wife; I wanted the "relationship building" of a phone conversation. He bought from a competitor who simply answered his email thoroughly. My preference had cost me the sale because I'd prioritized my comfort over his convenience.

Eliza built her communication approach around customer preference rather than her own. When customers reached out via text, she responded via text unless the complexity required a phone call—and then she'd ask permission first: "This might be easier to explain over the phone. Would you prefer I call you, or should I send a detailed text?" That simple question demonstrated respect for their time and communication style.

The Technology That Enables Seamless Integration

Effective omnichannel communication requires systems that connect your various touchpoints.[127][132] Eliza used her dealership's CRM to log every interaction—whether it came through text, email, phone, social media, or in person—so she could reference previous conversations regardless of channel.[127][132] When Marcus texted his question, she could see his entire history: his initial Facebook inquiry three weeks earlier, the email exchange about financing options, the phone conversation about trade-in value, and his in-person test drive.

This continuity transformed the customer experience. Marcus never had to repeat himself or wonder if Eliza remembered previous discussions.

Each interaction built on the last, creating momentum toward the sale rather than the frustrating restarts that happen when communication channels don't connect.[127][128]

The practical implementation doesn't require expensive enterprise software. Eliza started with a simple spreadsheet tracking customer names, preferred contact methods, conversation summaries, and next steps. As her business grew, she upgraded to a CRM system, but the principle remained constant: every touchpoint gets documented so the next interaction can reference it, regardless of which channel the customer chooses.[127][132]

Consistency Across Channels Without Robotic Repetition

The challenge of omnichannel communication is maintaining consistency while adapting your style to each medium's strengths.[128][130] Your email voice should feel like the same person as your text messages and phone conversations, but each channel has different expectations. Emails can be more detailed and formal. Texts should be concise and conversational. Phone calls allow for nuance and real-time problem-solving. Social media requires public-appropriate professionalism since others are watching.

Eliza's approach was to keep her core message consistent—helpful, honest, customer-focused—while adjusting format to the medium.[128][130] Her texts were brief but warm: "Great question about the safety features! Here's a quick video that shows exactly how it works: [link^. Let me know if you want to see it in person!" Her emails provided more detail with the same friendly tone.[127][128] Her phone conversations maintained the same authenticity as her written communication. Customers experienced her as genuinely herself across every channel, which built trust that transcended any single interaction.[128][132]

The salespeople who succeed with omnichannel communication understand that technology enables relationships rather than replacing

148

them.[127 130] Every text, email, social media message, phone call, and in-person conversation is an opportunity to demonstrate that you remember who they are, understand what they need, and genuinely care about helping them make the right decision—regardless of which channel they choose to reach you through.[127 130 132]

Post-Sale Relationship Maintenance: Systematic Follow-Up Strategies That Keep You Connected Without Being Intrusive

Two weeks after Daniel drove off in his new sedan, his phone buzzed with a text from Eliza: "How's the new car treating you? Any questions about features?" It was brief, personal, and genuinely helpful—not a sales pitch disguised as follow-up. Daniel responded with a question about the infotainment system, and Eliza sent a helpful video link within minutes. That thirty-second exchange represented the beginning of a systematic relationship maintenance strategy that would generate four referrals and two repeat purchases over the following three years.

The difference between intrusive follow-up and valuable relationship maintenance lies entirely in your intention and execution.[133 134] Customers can immediately sense whether you're checking in because you care about their satisfaction or because you're hunting for your next commission. The former builds loyalty; the latter destroys the trust you worked so hard to establish during the sale.

The Strategic Follow-Up Timeline

Effective relationship maintenance follows a predictable rhythm that aligns with the customer's ownership experience rather than your sales calendar.[133 136] Eliza developed a system that felt natural to customers because it connected to meaningful moments in their vehicle ownership journey.

Within forty-eight hours of delivery, she sent a personalized text checking in on their first impressions and offering to answer any questions.[134][139] This wasn't automated—she referenced specific details from their conversations, making each message genuinely personal.[133][134][135] Three weeks later, she sent a reminder about the first complimentary service appointment, including her direct contact to help schedule it.[135][136][137] At the three-month mark, she checked in again, asking how they were enjoying the vehicle and whether they'd discovered any features they particularly loved.

These touchpoints weren't arbitrary. Research on customer satisfaction shows that concerns typically surface within the first month, service appointments create natural engagement opportunities, and the three-month point represents when initial excitement settles into realistic ownership experience. By aligning her follow-up with these natural milestones, Eliza's outreach felt helpful rather than intrusive.

Adding Value Without Selling

The cardinal rule of post-sale relationship maintenance is simple: every contact should provide genuine value to the customer, not just create an opportunity for you to sell something.[133][134] When Eliza reached out at the six-month mark, she didn't ask if customers were ready to trade in—she shared a helpful article about seasonal maintenance tips relevant to their specific vehicle.[133][137] When she contacted customers on their vehicle's anniversary, she sent a personalized message celebrating their first year of ownership, not a pitch for an upgrade.

This value-first approach transformed how customers perceived her follow-up. Instead of dreading contact from "that salesperson trying to sell me something," they welcomed her messages because they'd learned she consistently provided useful information, answered questions promptly, and never pressured them toward unnecessary purchases.

I learned this principle through a painful mistake early in my career. I'd maintained good contact with a customer for eight months, then called her aggressively pushing a new model when she'd shown zero interest in trading. She told me bluntly, "I thought you cared about me as a person, not just as a commission source." That relationship never recovered, and I lost not just her future business but the three referrals she'd been planning to send my way.

Leveraging Technology Without Losing the Human Touch

The salespeople who excel at relationship maintenance use CRM systems and automation strategically—to ensure consistency and scale, not to replace genuine human connection.[133] [135] [136] [138] Eliza programmed her CRM to remind her of important customer milestones: birthdays, vehicle anniversaries, lease-end dates approaching. But she never sent automated messages that felt robotic or generic.

When her system flagged Daniel's daughter's birthday—a detail he'd mentioned during their initial conversations—Eliza sent a brief, personal text: "Hope your daughter has a great birthday today!" That fifteen-second effort generated a response from Daniel thanking her for remembering and mentioning that his wife was starting to research vehicles. That casual exchange led directly to his wife's purchase three months later.

The technology enabled Eliza to maintain relationships with hundreds of customers systematically, but her personal touch in every interaction made each customer feel individually valued.[133] [135] That combination— systematic consistency powered by technology, delivered with authentic human care—creates relationship maintenance that customers appreciate rather than avoid, building the foundation for referrals, repeat business, and the sustainable career success that comes from genuine loyalty rather than constant prospecting.

Leveraging Technology for Relationship Building: CRM Systems, Automated Touchpoints, and Digital Tools That Enhance Rather Than Replace Human Connection

When Sarah joined Eliza's dealership team, she brought a confession that many veteran salespeople share privately but rarely admit publicly: "I'm terrible with technology. I still write customer information on index cards." Eliza smiled, recognizing her former self. Three years earlier, she'd resisted her dealership's new CRM system, convinced that her personal notebook and memory were superior to "some computer program." That resistance had cost her two significant sales when customers slipped through the cracks of her manual tracking system.

The breakthrough came when Eliza reframed how she thought about technology. These tools weren't replacing her relationships—they were amplifying her ability to maintain them at scale.[14][17] A CRM system wasn't a cold database; it was a memory aid that ensured she never forgot a customer's daughter's birthday, a follow-up promise, or the specific concerns they'd expressed six months earlier.[14] Automation wasn't impersonal; it was the scaffolding that freed her to focus on genuinely personal interactions when they mattered most.[14][17]

CRM Systems: Your Relationship Memory Bank

The most successful salespeople I've encountered use CRM systems as extensions of their commitment to customers rather than administrative burdens. When Marcus texted Eliza about a service question fourteen months after his purchase, she pulled up his profile instantly: his vehicle details, his previous concerns about a specific feature, his mention of planning a cross-country trip, even his preference for text communication over phone calls. That context transformed a simple service question into a relationship-deepening conversation where Marcus felt genuinely remembered and valued.[14]

The practical implementation starts simply. Every customer interaction—whether a showroom conversation, phone call, text exchange, or email—gets logged with key details: their stated needs, family situation, timeline, concerns raised, and promises made.[14] This isn't bureaucratic paperwork; it's relationship insurance. When you contact that customer three months later, you're not starting from zero—you're continuing a conversation they'll remember you cared enough to track.[14]

Sarah initially struggled with this discipline until Eliza showed her the financial impact. By tracking every customer systematically, Eliza had generated twenty-three repeat purchases and forty-one referrals over two years—business that would have evaporated without consistent follow-up enabled by her CRM.[14] Sarah began logging details religiously, and within six months, she recovered three "lost" customers who'd been ready to buy but had fallen through her manual tracking cracks.[14]

Automated Touchpoints: Consistency Without Robotics

The key to effective automation is programming systems to remind you to be human, not to replace your humanity.[14][17] Eliza configured her CRM to alert her to customer birthdays, vehicle anniversaries, and service milestones—but she never sent automated generic messages.[14] When the system flagged Daniel's daughter's birthday, Eliza sent a personal text referencing their previous conversation about his daughter learning to drive. That fifteen-second effort, enabled by technology but delivered with authentic care, generated a response that led to his wife's vehicle purchase.[14][16]

Automation works best for routine touchpoints that maintain presence without demanding immediate response: service appointment reminders, seasonal maintenance tips, new inventory notifications for customers who'd expressed specific interests.[14] But the moment a customer responds, the interaction must become genuinely personal.[14][17] Technology creates the opportunity; your authentic engagement converts it into relationship depth.[16]

Digital Tools That Enhance Connection

The dealerships thriving in today's market use digital tools strategically to remove friction from customer relationships.[14][17] Eliza's text-based communication allowed customers to ask quick questions during their lunch breaks without the commitment of a phone call.[17] Her Facebook group created community among her customers, where they helped each other with vehicle questions while strengthening their connection to her.[14] Her video messages—thirty-second personalized clips thanking customers or answering specific questions—delivered human warmth through digital channels.[14][17]

The principle underlying all effective technology use in relationship building is simple: these tools should make it easier for customers to connect with you, easier for you to remember and honor what matters to them, and easier to maintain consistent contact that demonstrates genuine care.[14][17] Technology that serves those purposes enhances relationships. Technology that creates barriers, feels impersonal, or prioritizes efficiency over empathy damages them.[14][17][16] The salespeople who master this distinction build sustainable careers where digital tools amplify rather than replace the human connection that remains the irreplaceable foundation of automotive sales success.[14][17][16]

Building Your Sustainable Future in Automotive Sales

The transformation from transaction-focused selling to relationship-driven success isn't just a philosophical shift—it's a practical business model that generates measurably better results while creating a career you'll actually enjoy. Eliza's journey from skeptical newcomer to dealership sales director demonstrates what happens when you systematically implement the principles we've explored throughout this chapter: customer lifetime value thinking, authentic digital presence management, omnichannel communication integration, consistent post-sale relationship maintenance, and strategic technology leverage that enhances rather than replaces human connection.

The mathematics are undeniable. When you build your career on relationships that generate repeat business and referrals rather than constantly hunting for new prospects, your income becomes more stable, your work becomes less stressful, and your reputation compounds over time. Daniel's relationship with Eliza generated nearly six times the value of his initial purchase through repeat business and referrals—and he represents just one customer in a systematic approach that transforms every sale into the foundation of ongoing value creation. This isn't theory or wishful thinking; it's the documented experience of sales professionals who've discovered that genuine care for customer success creates sustainable financial success for themselves.

Your digital presence works for you around the clock, building credibility with prospects who arrive at your dealership already convinced you're someone they can trust because they've read your reviews, consumed your helpful content, and seen evidence that you prioritize customer relationships over quick commissions. Rachel's experience—researching

Eliza online, arriving pre-sold on her integrity, and completing her purchase in ninety minutes—represents the modern sales reality where your reputation precedes you and trust transfers digitally before you ever shake hands in person. The sales professionals who resist building authentic digital presence aren't protecting themselves from technology's impersonal nature—they're surrendering market share to competitors who understand that today's customers research people as thoroughly as they research vehicles.

The integration of systematic relationship maintenance with smart technology use creates something powerful: the ability to maintain genuine connections with hundreds of customers without anyone feeling like a number in a database. Your CRM system remembers birthdays, tracks promises made, and flags follow-up opportunities—but you deliver every interaction with authentic human care that makes customers feel individually valued. This combination of technological consistency and personal touch transforms your customer base from a list of past transactions into a community of advocates who generate referrals, return for future purchases, and provide the stability that insulates you from market fluctuations and inventory challenges.

The choice you face isn't whether to adapt to modern automotive sales realities—it's whether to adapt proactively or be forced to adapt reactively when traditional approaches stop generating results. The dealerships and sales professionals thriving today are those who recognized years ago that customer empowerment through digital information, social media transparency, and online reviews had fundamentally changed the game. They built relationship-focused businesses supported by digital tools rather than fighting against the tide of technological change.

As you move forward in your automotive sales career, remember that every customer represents a decision point: treat them as a one-time transaction or as the beginning of a relationship that compounds over time. The immediate commission might look the same either way, but the long-term trajectory of your career depends entirely on which choice you make consistently. The sales professionals who build sustainable success understand that their most valuable asset isn't their closing techniques or product knowledge—it's their reputation for genuine care, maintained through systematic relationship building, authentic digital presence, and the recognition that technology enables rather than replaces the human connection that remains the irreplaceable foundation of automotive sales excellence.

Conclusion

I still remember my first day on a dealership floor over two decades ago, walking into an environment that felt more like a battlefield than a place of business. The veterans around me spoke in terms of "conquering" customers, "overcoming" objections, and "closing" deals with the same intensity you'd use to describe a military operation. I watched salespeople deploy tactics that made customers visibly uncomfortable, saw managers celebrate transactions that left buyers with obvious regret, and witnessed an approach to selling that treated every interaction as a zero-sum game where someone had to lose.

That world is dying, and good riddance.

What you've read in these pages isn't just a collection of techniques or strategies—it's a fundamentally different philosophy about what automotive sales can and should be. The transformation from high-pressure tactics to relationship-driven success isn't happening because salespeople suddenly developed consciences. It's happening because the market demands it. Today's digitally-informed customers arrive with research, options, and platforms to share their experiences. They can smell manipulation from across the showroom, and they have infinite alternatives when they encounter it.

But here's what I've learned through thousands of customer interactions, countless training sessions, and years of watching both struggling and thriving sales professionals: the death of manipulative tactics isn't a loss—it's an opportunity. The salespeople who mourn the "good old days" of information asymmetry and pressure closes are missing something profound. Building genuine trust, understanding customer psychology, creating authentic rapport, adapting to digital realities, handling objections collaboratively, negotiating for mutual benefit, closing ethically, and maintaining long-term relationships isn't harder than the old way—it's actually easier, more profitable, and infinitely more sustainable.

Every story you've encountered in this book—from Ella's evolution beyond high-pressure tactics to Eliza's systematic relationship building—represents real patterns I've witnessed throughout my career. The names and details may be composites, but the fundamental truth remains: sales professionals who embrace relationship-driven approaches don't just survive in modern automotive retail—they dominate it. Their customer satisfaction scores soar. Their referral business becomes the foundation of sustainable income. Their careers get easier over time rather than harder because they're building on relationships that compound rather than constantly starting from zero with skeptical strangers.

If you're transitioning into automotive sales from another industry, you have an advantage: you haven't been conditioned by decades of dysfunctional practices. Bring your consultative skills, your relationship focus, and your ethical standards. They're not obstacles to overcome—they're your competitive edge. If you're a veteran looking to elevate your performance, I promise you this: the techniques in this book aren't "soft" approaches that sacrifice income for feel-good principles. They're the hardest-working strategies you'll ever implement, generating customer lifetime value that dwarfs what transactional selling ever could.

The automotive sales profession stands at a crossroads. One path leads backward to manipulation, pressure, and the adversarial dynamics that gave our industry its terrible reputation. The other leads forward to trust, partnership, and relationships that benefit everyone involved. The choice isn't just about ethics—it's about survival. The salespeople who choose the relationship-driven path will build careers that withstand market changes, economic fluctuations, and evolving consumer behaviors.

You now have the roadmap. The question isn't whether these strategies work—the evidence is overwhelming. The question is whether you'll implement them consistently, trust the process when it feels uncomfortable, and commit to building a career on relationships rather than transactions.

The showroom floor is waiting. Your customers are ready for someone different. Be that person.

Bibliography

References

[1] Wikipedia. (

[2] Klein, R.. (

[3] National Automobile Dealers Association. (

[4] LostDog. (November 18, 2021). *The Evolution of Car Salesmanship*. Curbside Classic. https://www.curbsideclassic.com/blog/editorial/the-evolution-of-car-salesmanship/

[5] DealersEdge. (2024, October 25). *A Brief History of the U.S. Auto Industry and the Evolution of Dealership Marketing*. DealersEdge. https://dealersedge.substack.com/p/a-brief-history-of-the-us-auto-industry

[6] Flammang, J. M.. (2022). *Clunkers & Creampuffs Chapter 16: Dealers Face Image Problem (1950s)*. Tirekicking Today. https://www.tirekick.com/Clunkers-Chapter%2016-Image.htm

[7] Car Dealership Guy. (2025, November 7). *The car sales secret lost in the 90's—and how dealers are reviving it at scale*. Dealership Guy.

https://news.dealershipguy.com/p/the-car-sales-secret-lost-in-the-90-s-and-how-dealers-are-reviving-it-at-scale-2025-11-07

[8] Marshall, C.. (2018, January 22). *Your Ad Budget Is Wasted. The Database Hustle Wins Every Time*. Auto Success Online. https://www.autosuccessonline.com/car-dealers-stuck-90s-live-chat-dealership-20-years-later/

[9] C-4 Analytics. (2025, August 21). *A Deep Dive Into the Evolution of Automotive Digital Marketing*. C-4 Analytics Insights. https://c-4analytics.com/insights/a-deep-dive-into-the-evolution-of-automotive-digital-marketing?hs_amp=true

[10] Zettelmeyer, F.. (2010, September 01). *A Decade of Change for the U.S. Auto Industry: The Internet, Promotions, and Rising Gasoline Prices*. The Reporter. https://www.nber.org/reporter/2010number3/decade-change-us-auto-industry-internet-promotions-and-rising-gasoline-prices

[11] truPayments. (2020, April 23). *The History of Automotive Digital Retailing*. shopbypayment.com. https://shopbypayment.com/2020/04/23/the-history-of-automotive-digital-retailing/

[12] Brown, J.. (2025, January 31). *Drive To Success: Mastering the Art of Auto Sales and Vehicle Exchange*. Barnes & Noble. https://www.barnesandnoble.com/w/drive-to-success-jinetta-brown/1146937825

[13] Brown, J.. (January 2025). *Drive To Success: Mastering the Art of Auto Sales and Vehicle Exchange*. ThriftBooks. https://www.thriftbooks.com/w/drive-to-success-mastering-the-art-of-auto-sales-and-vehicle-exchange_jinetta-brown/54779010/

[14] CBT News. (

[15] TailoredRead AI. (2025, May 9). *Driving Success: Advanced Strategies for Automotive Sales Leadership*. TailoredRead. https://tailoredread.com/book/driving-success-advanced-strategies-automotive-sales-5ddb67c75fd7

[16] Walker, B.. (2024, April 3). *Walker's Hierarchy of Marketing Needs*. Shop Marketing Pros. https://shopmarketingpros.com/walkers-hierarchy-of-marketing-needs/

[17] Schmitz, A.. (2012, December 29). *Psychological Factors That Affect People's Buying Behavior*. Marketing Principles. https://2012books.lardbucket.org/books/marketing-principles-v1.0/s06-04-psychological-factors-that-aff.html

[18] Chase, I.. (2025, March 25). *You have unmet needs: the psychology behind people's love of big cars*. Global English Editing. https://geediting.com/gb-you-have-unmet-needs-the-psychology-behind-peoples-love-of-big-cars/

[19] Taylor, F.. (2024, March 21). *7 Cognitive Biases that Influence Buyer Behavior and Decision-Making*. Lift Enablement. https://www.liftenablement.com/blog/7-cognitive-biases-that-influence-buyer-behavior-and-decision-making

[20] Caceres-Santamaria, A.. (2021, April 01). *The Anchoring Effect*. Federal Reserve Bank of St. Louis. https://www.stlouisfed.org/publications/page-one-economics/2021/04/01/the-anchoring-effect

[21] The Lab. (

[22] Rozange, F.. (2025, October 5). *The Trust Crisis in Automotive: Why the Industry Scored Lowest Among Consumer-Facing Sectors*. CSM Research. https://www.csm-research.com/the-trust-crisis-in-automotive-why-the-industry-scored-lowest-among-consumer-facing-sectors/

[23] Auto Remarketing. (2024, November 13). *Buyers trust dealers over private sellers, but are wary about hidden problems*. Auto Remarketing. http://digital.autoremarketing.com/articles/buyers-trust-dealers-over-private-sellers-but-are-wary-about-hidden-problems

[24] eLEND Solutions. (2023, October 10). *80% of Dealers Cite Lack of Lender Transparency as #1 Obstacle to Deal and Pricing Clarity*. eLEND Solutions. https://elendsolutions.com/press/lender-transparency-survey/

[25] Hartman, E.. (2024, February 22). *KPA Car Dealership Trust Survey: While A Minority of Americans Experience Deceptive Selling At Dealerships, Most Still Distrust Them*. KPA. https://kpa.io/blog/kpa-car-dealership-trust-survey-while-a-minority-of-americans-experience-deceptive-selling-at-dealerships-most-still-distrust-them/

[26] Staff Writer. (2024, October 28). *Trust Tops Price Among Auto Shoppers*. Used Car News. https://usedcarnews.com/index.php/component/k2/item/6769-trust-tops-price-among-auto-shoppers

[27] AutoAlert. (

[28] Lotlinx. (2024, June 20). *How to Build Trust and Credibility in the Digital Age of Auto Sales*. Lotlinx. https://lotlinx.com/how-to-build-trust-and-credibility-in-the-digital-age-of-auto-sales/

[29] Modera. (2024, December 7). *Car Sales Psychology – 11 Tips and Tricks to Sell Better in 2025*. Modera. https://modera.com/automotive/car-sales-psychology-11-tips-and-tricks-to-sell-better/

[30] Griffith, K.. (2020, October 29). *How Car Salespeople Can Build Trust*. University of Denver. https://www.du.edu/news/how-car-salespeople-can-build-trust

[31] Pinnacle Sales & Mail. (

[32] KB. (January 4). *Unleashing the Power of Active Listening in Car Sales.* Car Sales Professional. https://carsalesprofessional.com/unleashing-the-power-of-active-listening-in-car-sales/

[33] RevDojo. (2023, October 30). *Effective Communication on Car Sales: Clearly and Confidently Communicate the Value Proposition of the Cars You Are Selling.* RevDojo. https://www.revdojo.com/car-sales-communication

[34] Autocorp.ai. (December 5, 2024). *The Psychology of Car Sales: 15 Proven Tips (With Examples) to Sell Better in 2025.* Autocorp.ai. https://www.autocorp.ai/blog/the-psychology-of-car-sales-15-proven-tips-with-examples-to-sell-better-in-2025

[35]

[36] Staff Writer. (

[37] AutoAlert. (

[38] Jupiter Chevrolet. (2025, May 4). *Building Trust Through Transparency in Car Sales.* Jupiter Chevrolet. https://www.jupiterchev.com/blogs/6872/building-trust-through-transparency-in-car-sales

[39] Freedman, B.. (2024). *How Transparency Wins Business.* Dealer Magazine. https://read.nxtbook.com/digitaldealer/dealermagazine/julyaugustissueof dealerm/howtransparency_wins.html

[40] automotiveMastermind. (2021, February 12). *4 Ways for Dealerships to Create a Transparent Customer Experience.* automotiveMastermind.

https://www.automotivemastermind.com/blog/dealerships/4-ways-to-create-a-transparent-customer-experience/

[41] AutoRaptor Core. (

[42] Moaven Motors. (2024, July 16). *Selling Cars with Integrity: The Moaven Motors Way*. Moaven Motors. https://moavenmotors.com/bdp/46198/pre-owned-auto-sales-and-service/selling-cars-with-integrity-the-moaven-motors-way

[43] Lawrence, J.. (2023, June 16). *Transparency Triumphs: The Powerful Impact of Honesty when Selling Your Vehicle*. Luxe Automotive Vision. https://www.luxe.vision/transparency-triumphs-the-powerful-impact-of-transparency-when-selling-your-vehicle

[44] Dealertrack. (

[45] Ngiri, M.. (2025, August 9). *The Power of Transparency: Why Honesty Sells Cars*. WheelMax. https://www.wheelmax.ng/knowledge/articles/wm-the-power-of-transparency-why-honesty-sells-cars-2025-08-09-1754724293015

[46] Affinitiv. (2025, August 21). *5 Follow-Up Strategies That Keep Customers Coming Back*. Affinitiv. https://www.affinitiv.com/blog/5-follow-up-strategies-that-keep-customers-coming-back/

[47] Convin AI. (2025, February 18). *Best Way To Keep In Touch With Customers After They Visit My Dealership*. Convin AI. https://convin.ai/blog/automate-follow-ups

[48] eCarsTrade. (

[49] Automotive Training Network. (

[50] Market Doctors. (

[51] Brumberg, R.. (2024, March 8). *Online car buying statistics 2025.* ConsumerAffairs. https://www.consumeraffairs.com/automotive/online-car-buying-statistics.html

[52] Andersen, D.. (2025, March 3). *38 Statistics Automotive Marketers Need to Know in 2025.* Invoca. https://www.invoca.com/blog/automotive-marketing-statistics

[53] Salesforce. (2025). *Gen Z Takes the Wheel: Salesforce Research Shows Strong Demand for AI Agents in Younger Generations.* Salesforce News & Insights. https://www.salesforce.com/news/stories/gen-z-automotive-industry-stats-2025/

[54] LoudSpeaker Team. (2025, September 3). *32 Consumer Behavior in Car Buying Statistics in 2025.* Demand Local. https://www.demandlocal.com/blog/consumer-behavior-car-buying-statistics/

[55] Ullman, E.. (2025, June 18). *AI and virtual showrooms: The digital evolution of car sales.* WFTV. https://www.wftv.com/news/ai-virtual-showrooms-digital-evolution-car-sales/IHKYUTQRMFLGLOW73PZ6IMDSVY/

[56] Dietrichson, J.. (2025, March 5). *Dealerships Still Drive the Car Buying Experience in the Digital Age.* We Are Progressive. https://www.weareprogressive.com/insights/dealerships-still-drive-the-car-buying-experience-in-the-digital-age

[57] Pasch, G., & Ciociola, S.. (2025, March 26). *How lifecycle marketing transforms automotive sales.* CBT News. https://www.cbtnews.com/how-lifecycle-marketing-transforms-automotive-sales/

[58] Roessler, S.. (2021, October 15). *Transforming Automotive Sales Through CRM.* DriveCentric.

https://drivecentric.com/collection/transforming-living-rooms-into-showroom-floors

[59] Digital Dealership System. (

[60] Vaughan, T.. (2024, December 9). *Maximizing Automotive Sales: The Transformative Power of Digital Signage*. Poppulo. https://www.poppulo.com/blog/maximizing-automotive-sales-the-transformative-power-of-digital-signage

[61] Tao, C.. (2022, July 25). *7 Ways to Use Digital Signage for Automotive/Car Dealerships*. Kuusoft. https://www.kuusoft.com/blogs/7-ways-to-use-automotive-digital-signage-in-car-dealerships/

[62] DisplayNow. (2024, June 19). *How Car Dealership Digital Signage Can Improve Your Marketing Strategy*. DisplayNow. https://displaynow.io/blog/how-car-dealership-digital-signage-can-improve-your-marketing-strategy

[63]

[64] Autocorp.ai. (2024, September 10). *10 Common Sales Objections and How to Overcome Each of Them*. Autocorp. https://www.autocorp.ai/blog/10-common-customer-objections

[65] Lucido-Balestrieri, S.. (2025, November 12). *The Hidden Science Of Objection-Handling in Sales*. CloudTalk. https://www.cloudtalk.io/blog/the-hidden-science-of-objection-handling-in-sales/

[66] Badger Maps. (

[67] Taggart, S.. (2024, December 8). *CRUSHING SALES OBJECTIONS: Sam Taggart's Battle-Tested Tactics from the Trenches*. D2D Experts. https://thed2dexperts.com/overcome-sales-objections/

[68] Toussi, S.. (2024, July 24). *Turning No into Yes: Effective Objection Handling for Car Sales Professionals*. Digital Dealer. https://digitaldealer.com/news/turning-no-into-yes-effective-objection-handling-for-car-sales-professionals/160674/

[69] Pozniak, A.. (2025, March 12). *Objection Handling Framework: Develop a Routine to Increase Won Deals*. NetHunt CRM Blog. https://nethunt.com/blog/top-objection-handling-frameworks/

[70] Crane. (2025, September 24). *Stop Selling, Start Listening: Handling Objections The LAER Way*. Crane. https://crane.vc/stop-selling-start-listening-handling-objections-the-laer-way/

[71] Kessler, V.. (2024, August 5). *LAARC: A Guide to Effective Objection Handling in Sales*. Notch. https://www.notch.so/post/laarc-a-guide-to-effective-objection-handling-in-sales

[72] Vera, H.. (2022, April 25). *Use L-A-E-R For Objection Handling*. Sales Outcomes. https://salesoutcomes.com/use-laer-for-objection-handling/

[73]

[74] McQueen, A.. (

[75] Automotive Training Network. (

[76] W., T.. (

[77] RevDojo. (2021, October 01). *Overcome "The Price is Too High" Objections | Car Sales Training*. RevDojo. https://www.revdojo.com/overcome-the-price-is-too-high-objections-car-sales-training

[78] Handa-Oakley, B.. (2023, September 14). *Top 10 Objection Handling Training Techniques + Examples*. Retorio. https://www.retorio.com/blog/objection-handling-training

[79] Burdon, M.. (2025, April 2). *Objection Handling: 44 Common Sales Objections & How to Respond*. HubSpot Blog. https://blog.hubspot.com/sales/handling-common-sales-objections

[80] Bumble Auto. (

[81] Linkov, J.. (2025, March 26). *How to Effectively Negotiate the Price for Your Next New Car*. Consumer Reports. https://www.consumerreports.org/cars/car-pricing-negotiation/how-to-negotiate-a-new-car-price-effectively-a8596856299/

[82] Toussi, S.. (2025, July 9). *Mastering Negotiation: Winning Strategies for Car Dealers*. Digital Dealer. https://digitaldealer.com/news/mastering-negotiation-winning-strategies-for-car-dealers/165714/

[83] Program on Negotiation. (2013). *Win-Win Negotiation: Managing Your Counterpart's Satisfaction*. Program on Negotiation at Harvard Law School. https://www.pon.harvard.edu/daily/win-win-daily/win-win-negotiations-managing-your-counterparts-satisfaction/

[84]

[85] be *admin* new_2023. (2025, August 28). *Win-win negotiation strategies – Techniques and Examples*. Business Explained. https://business-explained.com/blog/win-win-negotiation-strategies-techniques-and-examples/

[86]

[87] Imparato, J.. (2024, March 6). *Building Dealer Profitability Through Pricing Transparency*. Market Scan.

https://www.marketscan.com/blog/building-dealer-profitability-through-pricing-transparency/

[88] Longo Toyota of Prosper. (2025, September 30). *Why is Transparent Pricing Important for Car Buyers?*. Longo Toyota of Prosper. https://www.longotoyotaofprosper.com/blogs/3123/car-tips/why-is-transparent-pricing-important-for-car-buyers/

[89] Boice, D.. (2025, May 5). *Why Transparent Pricing Can Make Or Break The Traditional Car-Dealership Model*. Team Velocity Marketing. https://teamvelocitymarketing.com/why-transparent-pricing-can-make-or-break-the-traditional-car-dealership-model/

[90] Glo3D.com Content Team. (2025, February 26). *How AI is Transforming Pricing Transparency for Car Dealerships*. Glo3D. https://glo3d.com/pricing-transparency-car-dealerships/

[91] TVI-MarketPro3. (2024, June). *Transparent Pricing in the Service Drive*. TVI-MarketPro3. https://www.tvi-mp3.com/blog/insights/transparent-pricing-in-the-service-drive/

[92] Neeley, S.. (2024, November 18). *How to Set Pricing Strategies That Attract More Buyers: A Step-by-Step Guide for Car Dealers*. Carketa. https://carketa.com/pricing-strategies-for-car-dealers/

[93] Yoast, J.. (2025, January 25). *Trade-In Secrets: Get More for Your Vehicle at Used Car Dealers*. United Auto Sales Saluda. https://united-saluda.com/blog/trade-in-secrets-get-more-for-your-vehicle-at-used-car-dealers

[94] Arkin, G.. (2025, August 29). *How Dealerships Determine Trade-In Value And How to Negotiate It*. Nexus Auto Transport. https://nexusautotransport.com/how-dealerships-determine-trade-in-value-and-how-to-negotiate-it/

[95] Lake Elsinore Honda. (2023, November 8). *Mastering the Art of Car Negotiation: A Comprehensive Guide*. Lake Elsinore Honda Blog. https://www.lakeelsinorehonda.com/blogs/5482/mastering-the-art-of-car-negotiation-a-comprehensive-guide

[96] Shefska, R.. (2025, June 3). *Car Trade in Tactics for Success*. CarEdge. https://caredge.com/guides/car-trade-in

[97] Barry, K.. (2025, February 19). *How to Beat the 'Four Square' and Other Car Dealership Sales Tactics*. Consumer Reports. https://www.consumerreports.org/cars/buying-a-car/beat-four-square-and-other-car-dealership-sales-tactics-a7590220303/

[98] Unhaggle. (

[99] NerdWallet. (2025, November 4). *Best Auto Loan Rates & Financing in 2025: Compare Lenders*. NerdWallet. https://www.nerdwallet.com/auto-loans/best/auto-loans-for-good-fair-and-bad-credit

[100] Consumer Financial Protection Bureau. (2022, November 08). *What are the different ways to buy or finance a car or vehicle?*. Consumer Financial Protection Bureau. https://www.consumerfinance.gov/ask-cfpb/what-is-the-difference-between-dealer-arranged-and-bank-financing-en-759/

[101] Orange County's Credit Union. (2021, September 13). *Financing a Car: Compare Your Options*. Orange County's Credit Union. https://www.orangecountyscu.org/stories/financing-a-car-dealerships-vs-big-banks-vs-credit-unions/

[102] Martin, A.. (2025, August 25). *What dealer financing is and how it works*. Bankrate. https://www.bankrate.com/loans/auto-loans/dealer-financing/

[103] Bank of America. (2025). *Where to get your car loan: Bank or dealer?*. Better Money Habits. https://bettermoneyhabits.bankofamerica.com/en/auto/car-loan-from-bank-vs-dealer

[104] Best Deal Auto Group. (

[105] Subramanian, G.. (2010). *Negotiation Advice for Buying a Car: Tips for Improving Your Negotiating Position*. Program on Negotiation at Harvard Law School. https://www.pon.harvard.edu/daily/business-negotiations/so-you-want-to-buy-a-car/

[106] Cox Automotive. (2018, July 30). *How to Convert on the 3 Customer Buying Signals*. Cox Automotive. https://www.coxautoinc.com/insights-hub/convert-on-customer-buying-signals/

[107] Antrim, S.. (2024, February 3). *What Are Customer Buying Signals?*. Lucidworks. https://lucidworks.com/blog/customer-buying-signals

[108] Attention. (

[109] Rhodes, A.. (2025, May 15). *11 Buying Signal Examples*. UserGems. https://www.usergems.com/blog/buying-signal-examples

[110] Novus Business Connections. (2023, September 17). *Buying Signals: What They Are And How To Spot Them*. Novus Business Connections. https://www.novus-bc.com/buying-signals/

[111] Lever, D.. (2024, January 14). *11 Buying Signals To Look Out For (Verbal & Non Verbal)*. Qwilr. https://qwilr.com/blog/sales-buying-signals/

[112] Korotaev, I.. (2025, August 24). *Auto Sales Tactics: Best Practices to Increase Dealership Conversions*. Debexpert.

https://www.debexpert.com/blog/auto-sales-tactics-best-practices-to-increase-dealership-conversions

113

[114] NIADA. (February 7, 2022). *10 tips to close more car deals*. NIADA. https://niada.com/dashboard/10-tips-to-close-more-car-deals/

[115] Reid, J.. (2021, Dec 20). *Whatever It Takes – Unless It's Snake Oil*. JM Reid Group. https://jmreidgroup.com/sales-ethics-whatever-it-takes/

[116] Harsh P.. (July 8, 2024). *15 Best Closing Techniques in Sales: Secrets to Closing Like a Pro!*. Alore. https://www.alore.io/blog/best-closing-techniques-in-sales

[117] Agarwal, N.. (2025, November 10). *15 Smart Sales Closing Techniques [Scripts and Examples]*. LeadSquared. https://www.leadsquared.com/learn/sales/sales-closing-techniques-scripts/

118

[119] W., T.. (

[120] AutoAlert. (

[121] Agarwal, N.. (2025, May 23). *21 Highly Effective Car Sales Scripts to Close More Deals*. LeadSquared. https://www.leadsquared.com/industries/automotive/automotive-car-sales-scripts/

[122] Girdner, J.. (2025, January). *Why Dealerships Must Embrace Omnichannel Communication for Sales Success*. TECOBI. https://www.tecobi.com/dealerships-omnichannel-communication-for-sales/

[123] Edelman, Z.. (2024, November). *The Role of Omnichannel Marketing in Car Dealership Success*. Fullpath. https://www.fullpath.com/blog/the-role-of-omnichannel-marketing-in-car-dealership-success/

[124] ActivEngage. (

[125] Bain & Company. (2021, October). *Cracking the code on automotive omnichannel sales*. Bain & Company. https://www.bain.com/insights/cracking-the-code-on-automotive-omnichannel-sales/

[126] automotiveMastermind. (December 8, 2023). *The Future of Automotive: Omnichannel Customer Experiences in 2024*. automotiveMastermind. https://www.automotivemastermind.com/blog/uncategorized/the-future-of-automotive-omnichannel-customer-experiences-2024/

[127] Uptima. (

[128] Automotive Training Network. (

[129]

[130] Younghusband, R.. (2023, February 17). *Top 10 Dealership Services Strategies That Yield Results*. Getac. https://www.getac.com/us/blog/dealership-services/

[131]

[132] Bowtie Auto Solutions. (

[133] Collins, C.. (2019, December 9). *Top 5 Customer Relationship Management Tools for Car Dealers*. Chris Collins Inc.. https://chriscollinsinc.com/sdr/top-5-customer-relationship-management-tools-for-car-dealers/

[134] GoTo. (2025, May 14). *From Showroom to Service Bay: Optimizing Customer Experiences*. GoTo. https://www.goto.com/blog/6-customer-experience-challenges-for-auto-dealerships

www.ingramcontent.com/pod-product-compliance
Lightning Source LLC
Chambersburg PA
CBHW072029290326
41934CB00012BA/3062